Al Kogut
2037 H
San Francisco

PRS- 7714

by

Sam Fry, JR.

HOW TO WIN AT BRIDGE

with Any Partner

GOLDEN PRESS · NEW YORK

With appreciation to

ALBERT LEVENTHAL and DON STERN

CONTENTS

Preface

Whether you are a sub-average bridge player, a good one, or a near-expert, it is entirely possible for you to pick up, in the course of a single year, hundreds of additional games and thousands upon thousands of additional points. A big statement, perhaps, but a true one.

You cannot achieve this happy result, however, by fiddling around with the "Schwenn-Zeckendorff System" or the "Zilch Response" or the "Golub-Jones Double" (which asks you to show the number of deuces and treys in your hand) or any one of a dozen other gadgeteering devices currently being sold to the American public. No, your only sure way to winning bridge is *to become a better partner*.

It is the basic purpose of this book to show you how to reach a closer understanding with the person who sits across from you at the table. And it doesn't much matter if that person is a total stranger, an international champion, or the fellow who rides back and forth with you on the commuting train five days a week. It is indeed possible—by the exercise of common sense and elementary logic and the use of a few down-to-earth tools of the game—to bring about a happy transformation in your bridge results.

By now, it is no secret to you that I deplore the present-day flood of artificial conventions and bidding gadgets. They wreck partnerships far oftener than they help them. How ludicrous it is to sit down at a table with a stranger and listen for fifteen minutes while he explains his "system" to you and then spend the next twenty minutes explaining yours to him. Such nonsense not only takes most of the fun out of the game but builds the partners up to a point of near hysteria where each expects the worst of the other—and almost always gets it!

The winning ways of the Italian International Team in the last few years have led American alarmists to label our methods as "antiquated." Significantly, most of these alarmists have their own system to peddle or a book to sell. The truth of the matter is that the Italians have been winning because they have played magnificently. As Albert Morehead pointed out in The New York Times, "Not only Italy but also France and Great Britain have teams that are likely to beat anybody. Yet there is nothing wrong with American bridge that American players really want to cure." In other words, "Gadgets had nothing to do with it"—to borrow Mae West's quote on goodness.

Certainly, as Mr. Morehead went on to point out, any rush by average-to-expert players to the Roman or Neapolitan Club System will end in disillusionment. The same is even more true of other trick methods, American, Italian or Cambodian.

I hope to convince you of two things in the pages of this book: First, the "system" used by 95 percent of America's leading players is still the best one to use. Second, intelligence and common-sense cooperation can enable you and your partner to win far more points.

Who's My Partner?

It just so happens you are sitting South and have been dealt this hand:

♠ A Q 7 6 2   ♡ K 10 8 5 4   ◇ K Q 3   ♣ None

The bidding has proceeded in this fashion:

EAST	SOUTH	WEST	NORTH
Pass	1 ♠	Pass	2 ♣
Dble	2 ♡	Pass	4 ♡
Pass	?		

What do you say now?

There are at least five conceivable actions: five clubs, five hearts, six hearts, pass, and four notrump. Most bridge books sort out the possibilities and tell you the first choice, second, and so on down the line. And that approach misses the entire point of successful *partnership* bridge.

There is only one answer to this bidding problem: *the best bid depends upon who your partner is.*

Five clubs is the standout call *provided* your partner is an experienced and level-headed player. Such a player easily recognizes this as a cue-bid rather than club support; he knows it invites a slam and promises first-round control in clubs. If he has a strong club holding—A-K, A-Q, or K-Q—he spots the duplication of values and concludes there is probably a gap in one of the other suits; therefore, he signs off at five hearts, declining your slam invitation. But let's say he has a cheesy club holding and compensating strength elsewhere. Ordinarily he'd be concerned about clubs, because East's double was "for business." But your cue-bid tells him you have the clubs locked up, and he knows his other values provide excellent slam material. So he is delighted to help you along—either by bidding five diamonds to show the ace (if he has it), or by jumping right to six hearts with good hearts (something like A-Q-x-x) and the king of spades.

6

But just try that five-club bid with an unimaginative player; he passes you like a shot. Five clubs probably goes down several tricks when the hand is cold for anything from five to seven hearts. Furthermore, he will blast you in the post-mortem: "I told you my full story, and you supported my suit, didn't you?" And to himself, "Besides, I play the hands better than you."

The truth of the matter is that some players sitting North are not capable of interpreting five clubs as a cue-bid. But all North has to do is listen to the bidding and think it out. East is a passed hand; he can't have much in hearts on this bidding; if he had only diamonds, he'd have overcalled in diamonds, instead of doubling. So East's double of two clubs can only mean he has good clubs behind North. Therefore South's five-club bid must show a *control*, not *length*.

It is pointless to try to explain all this to an uncomprehending partner. It is even more pointless to make a "perfect" bid with a glaringly imperfect partner. So you scrap the five-club bid and choose some other response: With an overbidder, you pass and hope you haven't missed a slam. With an underbidder, you bid six hearts and gamble that he has enough of the right cards. With a partner who prides himself on his guessing ability, you bid five hearts and pass the buck to him—his guess is likely to be as good as yours. Blackwood is no easy way out of this situation (as we shall see in Chapter 12); partner probably holds one ace, but the crucial question is *which* one? No matter which action you choose, it is better than risking a club contract.

The five-club bid would never occur to many players in the South position. Those that found the bid might, like as not, use it with the wrong partner. And that is the core of losing partnership tactics. We have all learned to handle certain combinations of cards in both the bidding and the play. But it is the rare player who even thinks about the handling of different combinations of players. Yet this is where the big dividends are.

If you play regularly with the same group of players and never vary your game when you cut a new partner, I guarantee you are throwing away at least 1000 points per session! If it is a semiweekly game, that adds up to well over 100,000 points a year—and it may run double that. Even if you are a consistent winner with constant tactics, you are chucking this total; you could win that much more.

Isn't it worth some effort to pick up these points?

The bits of evidence you need to play your players are everywhere around you. You need only learn how to recognize them and then make them work for you. When such an approach becomes a habit, you will have developed your own philosophy for winning.

There are two main areas, which might be called tools and tactics.

First, we will examine the tools. Essentially these are *bidding* tools. Just as pitching is conceded to be 70 per cent of winning baseball, so bidding is 70 per cent or more of winning bridge. As long as you get to reasonable contracts when your side has the cards, and stay out of trouble when you don't, you can hardly help winning.

It takes sound judgment to weigh all the variables and choose from among the available courses of action. Some hands lend themselves to scientific treatment—careful probes for the proper contract, exchanges of information until one partner can place the final contract intelligently. Other hands call for direct action, such as a leap to game or slam. I recommend the latter course frequently—even with good partners.

Is your bidding honest and reliable? Not 100 per cent of the time, we hope. Of course, you want to keep faith with your partner so he doesn't have to guess your holding. But you don't want your opponents to read you like an open book. At times your main objective is to fool the enemy —even if this also misleads your partner a bit.

You cannot decide which tool to use if you are not familiar with them all. This book will help you put all your tools in good working order.

Then you will be ready to adjust the gears so they mesh with your partner's to make the entire partnership mechanism function effectively.

This adjustment is largely a matter of bridge *tactics*.

The objective is *not* perfect bridge, for that is the surest way to losing bridge! Unless, of course, you happen to have a perfect partner.

You should aspire instead to play practical bridge. This means recognizing the limitations of the partnership and not overtaxing it. Once the objective is defined, the means follow logically. *Know Thyself* is the first step; *Know Thy Partner,* the second.

You will learn all you can about your partner's predilections—from what he states and what he does. When you know what he can and cannot do, you can adapt to his foibles and construct a winning partnership.

With a new partner, you keep the conventions few and simple. With a regular partner, you can indulge in more gadgets if you choose, although I strongly recommend simplicity here, too, as you shall see shortly.

The secret of winning tactics is to be aware of the difference between a hand in a newspaper or textbook and the same hand played at the table. When you read a bridge column, you consider only the cards and the bids. But at the bridge table there are three other people present—each with his own ideas of the game—and you are not just playing bridge, you are playing people.

8

System and Point Count

When two players sit down across from each other, whether for the first time or the hundredth, they must settle on a basic bidding system. I recommend to you the system played by about 95 per cent of our recognized leading players. I like to call it the "Standard American" system. Its basis was known to oldtimers as Culbertson; today it is thought of as Goren. Despite its early origins, this system is up-to-date because of the introduction of a few successful innovations.

It is the best all-purpose system for expert, average, and weak partners—for two champions playing an international match or for total strangers meeting at a bridge club, in a Pullman car, at a dinner party.

The beauty of this system is that it is both simple and flexible. A skilled partner can vary his tools and tactics with different partners and opponents. The system gives him room in which to maneuver; he is master of it, not a slave to rigid rules.

You can best be a good partner with this system. Use it intelligently, and you can win with any partner.

POINT COUNT

To the average player, unfortunately, "bidding system" is synonymous with point count. Originally point count was intended merely for hand evaluation—as a guide or supplement to the bidding structure. But many players, led on by some writers, have elevated it to a system.

Used in moderation, point count is an effective tool. A wee nip now and then is fine, but guzzle too much and you are a slave to the stuff.

Point count is certainly simple enough—4 points for an ace, 3 for a king, 2 for a queen, and 1 for a jack. If it were not so ridiculously easy, the point count would not have gained such wide acceptance.

Also, it is more accurate than the old Honor Trick method. With 40 points to a full deal, you obviously have a finer measuring stick than with a maximum of 10 Honor Tricks.

But point count is not the ultimate weapon. It is simple, but at the cost of greater accuracy. More accurate methods using half-points and quarter-points have been tried and discarded as too much trouble to learn. Accuracy has been sacrificed for simplicity. Thus you have a useful tool in point count, but not a perfect one.

As long as you consider only high-card points, point count is helpful in two areas of bidding:

1. *Notrump Bidding:* Point count solves almost all problems here. After hearing an opening one-notrump bid, responder knows his partner has a balanced hand with 15 to 18 points, and he is rarely at a loss what to do. The opener, if asked, can indicate whether he has a maximum or minimum, and the partnership lands in a reasonable contract.

   If you have a balanced hand after partner's opening *suit* bid, point count helps determine whether to respond in notrump and at what level. In fact, any time you hear your partner rebid or respond in notrump, point count provides a useful measuring stick.

2. *Opening Suit Bids of One:* It saves needless wear and tear on the gray cells to know that 14 or more high-card points constitute a compulsory opening bid, no matter how poor the distribution or how weak the best suit. When you can count only 12 points and don't have a really good suit or a fair two-suiter, you are alerted to pass. And it is equally valuable to know that you can only get in trouble by opening a hand like

   ♠ A K x x   ♡ x x x   ◇ 10 x x   ♣ A x x

   even if it does contain 3 old-fashioned Honor Tricks.

   You could work all this out for yourself, but point count is a safe short cut.

However, the point-count hucksters were not content to let well enough alone. They extended point-count valuation to distribution, doling out so many points for a short suit (or long suit, depending on which text you read). I simply can't see slide rules ever replacing common sense here. Bidding is too complex. There are too many variables—the sequence of the bidding, the action or silence of the opponents, the different deductions that can be drawn, the psychological and strategic considerations—that get in the way of any rigid mathematical formula for distribution.

If a player of some experience cannot logically value his distribution for what it is worth and make adjustments as the bidding unfolds, then he shouldn't play bridge. Point count cannot do the job for him.

I'll show just one example of this madness. How many points do you count for a suit of K-J-7-5-4-2? Opposite a void you will be lucky to win two or three tricks if this is your trump suit; at notrump you may take none. Opposite a singleton you may get two, three, or even four tricks at a trump contract; at notrump you may take none. Opposite a doubleton . . . and so on up the line.

I suggest you forget about memorizing point-count values for distribution. Instead, play more. Learn judgment from experience, by listening to the bidding carefully and trying to put the pieces together logically.

Keep point-count as a high-card guide for notrump and borderline opening-suit bids; use your head the rest of the time.

Opening One-Bids

A winning bridge player wants to get into the bidding whenever he can. If the hand belongs to his side, he wants to grab it. If it doesn't, there is still a chance to steal it—or at least make the bidding more difficult for his opponents. If nothing else, his opening bid may direct a favorable lead against the opponents' final contract.

Paradoxically, opening the bidding light is usually safer than overcalling on a sketchy hand. When you make an opening bid, the opponents do not yet know each other's strength; if they are to catch you red-handed, one must double for take-out and the other must be able to pass for penalties—a rare combination. But when you overcall, the next player can make a hair-trigger double since he knows his partner has values and his double won't be misunderstood.

You might think that because of this the experts would slash the requirements for an opening bid, but they don't—not for fear of the opponents, but for fear that partner may rely on the bid for full values and get the partnership up too high.

Once you fire the opening shot in a battle, you rarely have the chance to retire immediately. It is much easier to get into the bidding than out of it. Thus, when you are playing with an overbidder, it pays to tighten up your belt a notch. With a timid partner, you naturally let it out a little. This advice applies only to borderline hands; whenever you have a clear-cut bid or pass, you should make it, regardless of your partner-of-the-moment.

The more skilled the player, the fewer the borderline decisions. There is almost no such thing as an absolute toss-up. This becomes clear when you consider the baseball cliché "A tie favors the runner," which means that when ball and runner reach first base simultaneously, the runner is safe. But the fact is any big-league umpire on top of the play knows which arrived first—no matter how narrow the margin. What seems a tie to the fan is just a smaller margin to the ump.

The expert bridge player, like the umpire, is able to spot that narrow margin.

WHEN AND WHAT TO OPEN

There are three inter-related criteria for deciding when to open and what suit to bid:

1. *The strength of your hand.* You determine this from the point count and the presence or absence of a decent suit.

2. *Preparedness for a rebid.* Any new-suit response by a non-passed partner forces you to bid again, so you have to be prepared for this. You want to be able to show a second suit (if you have one) without getting too high, or to make a natural rebid without advertising more strength than you have.

3. *Your position at the table.* If you are third or fourth hand, your partner's pass has freed you from the obligation to rebid. You therefore may reduce a bit the requirements for an opening bid. On shaded third-hand openers, your bidding objective is different; you want to indicate a good lead for your partner, so you don't bother to show a mangy suit.

OPENING WITH ONE NOTRUMP

One notrump is the classic example of the prepared bid. It describes the strength and distribution of the hand within narrow limits; it tells practically the whole story at once. For that reason, the usual obligation for a rebid does not hold in this case. Responder sets the final contract; if he wants further information from the opener, he requests it.

The range of strength required for the strong* notrump is generally accepted as 16 to 18 points. Nobody promulgated these figures as doctrines, but experience has shown that hands within this range are difficult to handle if opened with one of a suit. If partner responds one of another suit, the hand is too good to rebid one notrump and not good enough to bid two notrump. Ergo, it is better to describe the hand at once with an opening one-notrump bid.

*As distinguished from the weak notrump—12 to 14 points—a highly specialized bid introduced by a small group of expert tournament players. It is reasonably effective at match point play, particularly against weak opposition, but very dangerous in a tough rubber bridge game.

To give this excellent tool more utility, I suggest you broaden the range to 15-18 points for all four table positions. A very bare 15 points without a single ten-spot or other plus value doesn't qualify (except possibly if you are not vulnerable against vulnerable opponents); on the other hand, a fat 18 points—with tens and nines—is too big.

The opening notrump bid always shows a balanced hand—a 4-3-3-3, 4-4-3-2, or 5-3-3-2 distribution. The doubleton generally should be no worse than Q-x, but occasionally you can get by with J-x or 10-x if the hand is otherwise suitable.

A 5-card suit is no bar to an opening one-notrump bid provided not too much of your strength is massed in the suit. However, if you also have 17-plus points or 18 high-card points, you are too strong for one notrump. The fifth card in a suit headed by a high honor combination is surely 1 point, and this brings you over the 18-point maximum.

Here are some typical opening one-notrump bids:

1. ♠ A J 7 5	♡ K 9 2	◇ K 8 7 3	♣ A J
2. ♠ 9 6 5	♡ A K 10	◇ A J 8 2	♣ K Q 3
3. ♠ Q 4	♡ A K 9 2	◇ K 9 4	♣ A 10 5 2
4. ♠ A 10 3	♡ K 7	◇ A J 8 6 2	♣ K J 9
5. ♠ K 4	♡ A Q 7 6 2	◇ A J 3	♣ Q 9 5

Now a few 15-pointers that qualify:

1. ♠ K 10 4	♡ Q 10 9 3	◇ A Q 7	♣ K J 5
2. ♠ J 6 5	♡ Q 10 4	◇ K Q 8 2	♣ A K 10
3. ♠ A J 10	♡ K 9 6 4	◇ A Q 10 2	♣ J 9
4. ♠ A Q	♡ K 10 6 3	◇ 9 7 6 2	♣ A Q 8

Let's examine next a few hands that do not quite qualify for an opening one notrump. However, you might elect to open these with a notrump for some unusual strategic reason or because your partner is a novice.

1. ♠ K Q 9   ♡ A Q 10   ◇ A J 8   ♣ Q 10 9 3
Bid one club. 18-plus points are too good for one notrump.

2. ♠ A K J 3   ♡ A Q J 2   ◇ 10 7 4   ♣ Q 4
Bid one spade. Strength is too concentrated in two suits.

3. ♠ A 10 3   ♡ Q 5 2   ◇ A K 7 3   ♣ J 10 2
Bid one diamond. Only 14-plus points.

4. ♠ A K   ♡ 10 7 6 3   ◇ K J   ♣ A Q 9 7 3

Bid one club. Game could be in clubs, hearts, or notrump, and you need more bidding room for exploration.

OPENING WITH ONE IN A SUIT

With less than 15-plus points or an unbalanced hand, you look for an opening suit bid. You are probably familiar with the compulsory 14-high-card-point opener and 12-to-13-point hands with distributional features, so a very few examples will suffice:

1. ♠ K J 8   ♡ 10 4   ◇ A Q 6 4   ♣ A 5 4 2

Bid one diamond. 14 high-card points, a convenient biddable suit, and no flaws.

2. ♠ A 5   ♡ K Q 10 7 3   ◇ K 7 4   ♣ J 3 2

Bid one heart. 13 points plus a rebiddable suit.

3. ♠ A J 10 6 4 3   ♡ K Q 9 5   ◇ J 4   ♣ 6

Bid one spade. Only 11 points, but a fine 6-card major suit, good distribution, and strength in the other major.

Here are a few borderline situations:

1. ♠ A 7 3   ♡ A 7 4 2   ◇ A 3 2   ♣ J 5 2

Pass, except with an ultraconservative partner. 13 high-card points, but bad distribution, a heart suit you are ashamed of, and a club suit too anemic for opening a prepared short club.

2. ♠ A K 6   ♡ Q 8 6 2   ◇ 7 6 4 3   ♣ K J

Pass, unless you have a timid partner. You have 13 points, but no convenient rebid.

3. ♠ A K 6   ♡ Q 8 6 2   ◇ 9 6 3   ♣ K J 9

Bid one club. The extra club makes all the difference. Now you can rebid at the one level and can stand a club lead if the opponents buy the hand.

4. ♠ K 10 5   ♡ K J   ◇ A 10 4 3   ♣ Q 8 6 2

Bid one diamond, planning to rebid one notrump over any one-level response.

5. ♠ A 7 2   ♡ Q 8 4   ◇ A Q 6 4 3   ♣ 10 4

Bid one diamond with any partner. Only 12 points, but a 5-card suit in a hand with two aces.

6. ♠ 7 4   ♡ Q 8 2   ◇ A Q 6 4 3   ♣ A 6 2

Bid one diamond, but a pass is reasonable except when partner is a distinct underbidder. This is a close one. You have almost the identical strength and distribution of Hand 5, but Hand 5 has support in both majors, increasing the chances for a major-suit game. Here you have a worthless doubleton spade.

THIRD AND FOURTH HAND

Freed of the obligation to rebid, you may open lighter third and fourth hand. Partner's pass combined with your shaded or minimum opener tells you when a game is most unlikely, so you can pass certain of his responses without feeling too guilty.

You open certain hands in third position even if you know the enemy has most of the high cards and will very likely outbid you. Your objective is to get a favorable opening lead from partner or to make life difficult for the opponents. But fourth hand, you pass such hands like a flash.

A few illustrations:

1. ♠ K 10 4   ♡ K 10 9 3 2   ◇ K 8 3   ♣ Q 4

Bid one heart third or fourth hand and pass partner's response. You have just enough strength for a better-than-even chance to get a plus score. Better pass, however, with a bullish partner who will take you too seriously.

2. ♠ A K Q 8   ♡ 6 5 4   ◇ Q J 2   ♣ 10 9 3

Bid one spade third hand; pass fourth hand unless Mrs. Milquetoast is your partner. You have some chance of buying this hand and surely have an excellent opening lead to offer.

3. ♠ Q 7 3   ♡ 10 7 4 2   ◇ K Q J 6 5   ♣ 4

Pass fourth hand; *bid one diamond* third hand if non-vulnerable against vulnerable opponents. If both sides are non-vulnerable, you judge your personnel and take your chances. Call this a psychic, if you will, but it can work beautifully and shouldn't hurt you. This bid may keep the opponents from bidding three notrump—or set them if they get there.

CHOOSING THE SUIT

Most hands that qualify for an opening bid offer a choice of suits. Choose the bid that makes subsequent action easier for both partner and yourself.

Don't burden yourself with too many restrictions in this all-important area of bidding. The more don'ts you have, the less your opportunity for anticipation and the more wooden your bidding.

For that reason I do not subscribe to the cult of players who refuse to open a 4-card major suit in first or second position. Most expert opinion is with me on this point. A good many players experimented with the 5-card-major idea way back in the early 1930's (some even based an entire bidding structure on it) and discovered it didn't work.

However, I will not bid a bad 4-card major—one any weaker than, say, K-J-x-x. And usually I want something stronger, unless I am just strapped for a bid.

If you cut a partner who kneels at the 5-card-major altar, don't get in a hassle with him. Tell him that you'll count on him for a 5-carder but that you may occasionally bid a *good* 4-card major.

Common sense and anticipation, not ironclad rules, will solve most of your bidding problems. To illustrate this, I have selected twenty sample hands that run the gamut of situations and offer a sensible approach to them:

1. ♠ 7 6   ♡ K Q J 7   ◇ K Q 6 2   ♣ A 5 4
Bid one heart. This hand illustrates the weakness of the 5-card-major school. The heart suit, although only four cards, can stand on its own and play opposite three small ones if need be. However, even if your partner has four cards to the eight-spot or three to the ace, he's not going to bid them if you don't. If partner responds one spade, you bid one notrump; if he responds two clubs, you bid two diamonds.

2. ♠ 3   ♡ A K 9 4   ◇ 10 7 3 2   ♣ A Q J 8
Bid one heart. The suit is surely respectable enough. If partner responds one spade, as you anticipate, you bid one notrump or two clubs.

3. ♠ 10 7 3 2   ♡ A K 9 4   ◇ 3   ♣ A Q J 8
Bid one club. This hand is identical to Hand 2 except spades and diamonds are reversed. If you open with a heart, a two diamond response will prove embarrassing. But the club opening takes care of all contingencies; over one diamond you show the hearts; if partner's response is one spade, you raise to two.

4. ♠ A 5   ♡ K 9 8 3   ◇ K Q 4 2   ♣ Q 9 4
Bid one diamond. The heart suit is a jack short of our minimum. The only awkward response for you is two clubs, but since this would show definite strength, you would then be safe in bidding two notrump.

5. ♠ 8 3   ♡ 9 5 4   ◇ A Q 8 4   ♣ A K 4 2
Bid one diamond. The general rule is to prefer the higher-ranking of two touching suits of equal length.

6. ♠ A K J 9 ♡ A Q J 6 ◊ J 7 4 ♣ 10 6
Bid one spade. You intend to bid both majors since both are strong, so there is no point to a short-minor-suit opening.

7. ♠ K J 4 2 ♡ A Q J 6 ◊ A 7 5 4 ♣ 3
Bid one heart. Your spade suit is a bit shabby, and partner can easily bid the suit, if he has it, over your one-heart opener and you will be happy to raise. If he responds one notrump or two clubs, you bid two diamonds.

8. ♠ K 8 6 3 ♡ A J ◊ A Q 7 2 ♣ 9 5 2
Bid one diamond. Again, the spades are not robust enough to show on your own, but if partner responds in spades, you will raise. Over one heart bid one spade, and over two clubs you need not be ashamed of a two-notrump bid.

9. ♠ A K 7 5 ♡ 6 4 3 ◊ 9 2 ♣ A Q 10 3
Bid one club. This is a prepared bid. Over the expected red-suit response you comfortably rebid one spade. If you open one spade, a red-suit response forces you to bid clubs at the three level.

10. ♠ K Q J 5 ♡ 7 ◊ A Q 10 5 ♣ Q 7 6 3
Bid one diamond. Choose the suit "under the singleton" on 4-4-4-1 hands, and your rebids will almost always be easier. You are not ashamed of your spades; on the contrary, you hope to show them over the expected one-heart response.

11. ♠ A 10 ♡ K J 10 9 ◊ A Q 10 8 6 ♣ 9 5
Bid one heart. You can now comfortably rebid in diamonds. But if you open one diamond and then show the hearts, you will arrive at the three level or game willy-nilly. Your major duty here is to describe the overall strength of the hand.

12. ♠ K Q 10 6 ♡ A J 7 5 2 ◊ K 4 ♣ 7 3
Bid one spade. If you begin with the longer heart suit, you will face the choice of either keeping silent about the spades or else making the frightful rebid of two spades, which promises far more strength than you have here. This is the same situation as in Hand 11.

13. ♠ A K Q J ♡ K 4 ◊ 10 3 ♣ Q 9 6 4 2
Bid one club. Prefer the 5-card club holding, despite the great spade strength. This differs from Hands 11 and 12, because the club and spade suits are *not touching.* You anticipate a one-level response over which you can conveniently show the spades.

14. ♠ A 8 4 2 ♡ K Q 10 4 2 ◊ K 5 ♣ 8 6
Bid one heart. The spades are not sturdy enough to open and you do not intend to show both majors yourself, so it rests with partner whether spades are the

eventual trump suit. You will rebid hearts over a minor-suit response, but will, of course, raise spades if given the chance.

15. ♠ K J 9 4   ♡ A 7 5 4 2   ◇ A Q 5   ♣ 3
Bid one spade. A close one, and I would not quarrel with the one-heart bidders. However, the spade holding fulfills the minimum requirement, and the heart suit is not really rebiddable. Prefer to show both majors on this hand; if you open with one heart, you have an awkward choice over a one-notrump or two-club response.

16. ♠ K Q 7 3   ♡ 10 8 6 5 2   ◇ A K   ♣ 10 3
Bid one spade. The same considerations apply here as in Hand 15, but the spades are a bit better and the hearts are worse.

17. ♠ K 10 6 3   ♡ A 10 8 4   ◇ Q 7   ♣ A J 3
Bid one club. Here is the famed "short" club. Neither major suit is good enough to open, but you want to give partner a chance to respond in either at the one level. The hand is a point under an opening notrump.

18. ♠ J 8 6 2   ♡ K 7 3   ◇ K Q 3   ♣ K Q 6
Bid one club. Here again you have to bid the short club, because there is no other suit worthy of mention.

19. ♠ A 10 3   ♡ K 9 5 4   ◇ A K 9   ♣ 10 9 3
Bid one diamond. Again a short-suit minor, but this time you choose diamonds as you have more strength there and can stand the lead.

20. ♠ 9 7 4   ♡ A Q 2   ◇ Q 8 7 3   ♣ A Q 3
Bid one diamond. Prefer the 4-card minor suit, even if the clubs are stronger.

THE SHORT CLUB

Note that the controversial short club (or diamond) appears in only three of our twenty illustrations. Nonetheless, a few words of caution are in order:
- Never bid it on fewer than three cards.
- The suit should be headed by an ace or king, very rarely the queen; you must be ready to some extent to receive a lead in the suit.
- Don't ever tell your partner that you play a short club. It is not a convention on which to build a bidding system. It is just a convenience, used very infrequently.

Some players are deathly afraid that to bid a short club without prior agreement is to court the disaster of a raise on a 3-card holding. It just doesn't happen! If partner has only three clubs, he must have four cards in another suit, and will either show it at the one level or else respond one notrump. Therefore, with any reasonably intelligent partner you can count on at least four cards whenever he can find no better bid than a club raise.

THIRD AND FOURTH HAND

We have seen that the decision whether to open the bidding is influenced by the fact that your partner has already passed. The choice of which suit to open is also affected. In third or fourth position you should bid only suits of real muscle on minimum hands. There is a good chance the enemy will outbid you, and you don't want partner to sacrifice a trick by leading into some dog-eared suit you have scraped up.

Furthermore, you steer away from the short club on marginal third- and fourth-hand openers; there is no point in making such a prepared bid now that you are allowed to pass partner's response. You might make an exception when you have an ultra-conservative partner who passes big hands; you may decide to bid twice in hopes partner will come to life, and it is more convenient to start with a club.

A few examples:

1. ♠ A Q J 2   ♡ Q 3   ◇ 7 4 2   ♣ A 7 6 2
Bid one spade in third or fourth position. You would open one club first or second hand, so you could show your spades over a red-suit response. But with a passed partner, one spade offers a better lead and has more pre-emptive value. You plan to pass if partner makes a non-jump response.

2. ♠ K Q 8 6   ♡ J 10 2   ◇ 10 5 4   ♣ A K 3
Bid one spade third or fourth hand. You would open a short club first or second hand, but this is unnecessary here because you do not plan to rebid.

3. ♠ 9 6 4 3 2   ♡ A K J 9 8   ◇ Q 5   ♣ 5
Bid one heart. Forget about the spades, since you do not intend to bid again. You certainly don't want a spade lead, and it looks as though the opponents will play this hand.

UNBALANCED HANDS

When you are blessed with two 5-card suits, you should first bid the higher-ranking, regardless of which is stronger. The one exception is noted in Hand 4.

1. ♠ Q 10 6 5 2   ♡ A K J 4 2   ◇ K 5   ♣ 3

Bid one spade, despite the stronger heart holding. You will surely show your hearts on the next round.

2. ♠ A 10 8 3 2   ♡ Q 4   ◇ K Q J 6 3   ♣ 4

Bid one spade. Over two clubs you can bid the diamonds; over two hearts you must be content with a mere two-spade rebid. You don't relish suppressing the diamond suit on this sequence, but it is more important to explore the major-suit possibilities and avoid a bad overbid.

3. ♠ A 10 8 6 2   ♡ A 5   ◇ K Q J 8 3   ♣ 4

Bid one spade. Same as Hand 2, but this time you are good enough to bid three diamonds over a two-heart response.

4. ♠ A Q 7 5 3   ♡ K 5   ◇ 4   ♣ K J 10 6 2

Bid one club. Experience has shown that one club works out best when you hold five cards in both black suits. This is the one exception to the rule noted above. You show your spades on the next round and, depending on the course of the bidding, may rebid them later.

With both a 6-card and a 5-card suit, you almost always bid the longer suit first and rebid the 5-carder. If you mention the higher-ranking suit first, partner cannot always be sure whether you have 5-5 or 6-5. However, if your 6-card suit is the lower-ranking, he can figure you for 6-5 with reasonable certainty. The one exception is the club-spade holding given above.

1. ♠ A Q 7 6 5   ♡ 5   ◇ A K 7 4 3 2   ♣ 8

Bid one diamond. You intend to bid and rebid spades to show your 6-5 distribution.

2. ♠ A K J 7 4   ♡ K 7 6 4 3 2   ◇ 4   ♣ 7

Bid one spade. An exception. It is the weakness in hearts even more than the strength in spades that should persuade you to suppress showing the 6-5 holding clearly. If you open hearts and then bid spades twice, you will be arbitrarily taking the hand to game. You're better off starting with a spade so that partner can show a preference at a lower level.

If you carefully select your opening bid, you rarely find yourself stuck as the auction progresses. You glide into reasonable contracts oftener and with greater assurance. That is, if you have a sensible partner. But if you have an eccentric across the table, it is perhaps even more important to start the bidding on the right foot to avoid any wild flights into the danger zone.

Gadgets and Gadgeteers

Systems do not make good bridge players; it's just the reverse.

Anybody can invent a bridge bidding system—and a playable one at that. If you taught two fairly bright nine-year-old youngsters the rudiments of contract bridge, I wager that within a few weeks they could devise their own bidding system. If two ranking experts adopted it, practiced with it, and embellished it a bit, they would win tournaments with it. But, of course, these same experts would also win tournaments without the nine-year-olds' system.

Most bridge players play the game for fun. Unless they are eccentric or have a superabundance of free time, they don't bother to invent a new system, especially since there already is a top-notch one that is known, more or less, to all prospective partners.

But some experts are never satisfied and are constantly trying out new ideas. I am all for progress, but I wish these impassioned innovators would wait until they have come up with something genuinely useful for masses of players before selling it far and wide.

A number of fringe systems have obtained some following in recent years. But I assure you their publicity far outweighs their utility—and, fortunately, their popular acceptance, as well.

This book is dedicated to promoting winning partnership bridge, but before we can go ahead with this I must clear away some of the debris. After all, learning how to play winning bridge is as much a matter of discarding the frivolous as adopting the practical. If I seem to be destructive now and then and strike out with vigor at certain modern tendencies, it is only because these things must be stated—and shouted, rather than whispered in craven fear. If I offend a few of our leading lights, it is with the sincere conviction that the methods I recommend are effective and theirs fall short of the mark.

Some years ago, when P. Hal Sims was in his heyday, the Sims System received a great deal of publicity and thousands of players went along for the ride. There was no real merit in the Sims System, but there was much real bridge ability in Hal Sims and a few of his regular partners.

The Sims System died out, but everywhere around us are other fringe systems; those with considerable acceptance include the Roth-Stone and Kaplan-Sheinwold systems.

The Roth-Stone System is characterized by a reluctance to enter the bidding early with a light opening bid, overcall, or "free" response. This is a method for geniuses. We don't want to be forced to guess, at a higher, more dangerous level, whether to back into the bidding.

The Kaplan-Sheinwold System is built primarily on the weak notrump bid. This has not proved itself to my satisfaction; furthermore, it is dynamite in the hands of any but very expert players. Undismayed, the Messrs K. and S. seem to improvise at the rate of one new gadget per week.

Then, of course, there are the Neapolitan and the Roman systems employed so successfully by the Italian teams. Both are complicated and replete with artificial bids. Having played against both systems in international matches, I have concluded it is the excellence of the Italian players that makes their systems so successful, not vice versa. The captain of the Italian team likens these systems to high-powered, delicately tuned racing cars—fine for championships but not for everyday driving.

In fairness, I want to add that many of these concoctions have merit and are playable. However, they are designed for specialized, experienced, and very well-practiced partnerships. Some are particularly effective against weaker opponents, but do not fare well against equally strong opponents.

Furthermore, most of these gadget systems are designed for matchpoint duplicate play, and they ignore the realities of money or rubber bridge. If a gadget misfires at match points, it costs only a bottom in one hand out of many, but at rubber bridge it may hurt 2000 points worth. The rigidity of many of these methods makes no allowance for a change in tactics because of the relative abilities of partner and opponents.

Gadgets are usually difficult to memorize and mighty easy to forget at a crucial moment. I am no lazier than the next player, but I see little point in working so hard to master any system that will strait-jacket me.

ARTIFICIAL BIDS AND GADGETS

In general, I am opposed to artificial bids. It goes against my grain when somebody bids diamonds to mean one of any number of things—except that he has diamonds. Pig Latin is for teenagers; secret codes, for little boys playing G-men; and most gadgets, for the birds.

Once, in a wild fury over artificial bids, I came out with one of my own: the Fry opening two-heart bid. It is to be used only in second or fourth position to show the following hand:

♠ A Q 7 4 2   ♡ 6 3   ◇ A 9 8 4   ♣ K 3

A *few* artificial bids serve a highly useful purpose and have had general acceptance for many years. I warmly embrace them and will deal with them in subsequent chapters.

But most artificial bids are just play toys foisted on the bridge public by experts and pseudo-experts. After all, if you can't get a vaccine named after you, like Dr. Salk, you can at least settle for a bidding convention as your vehicle to immortality. These tricky little bidding devices attempt to do too much; when you graft them onto an integrated system, the whole structure becomes unwieldy and complex. Every time you give a bid a new and unusual meaning, you lose the chance to use the bid naturally. The chief characteristic of most of these gadgets is that they ask a question rather than give information. My rather intemperate reaction to most of those asking bids is "None of your business; bid your own hand, and let me bid mine."

What are the gadgeteers doing to the game? To give you just a glimpse of the terrain, I've summarized the official convention listing of the American Contract Bridge League way back in September 1958. The latest figures are much higher, with the upstate returns still coming in:

37 conventions . . . must be allowed in tournament play
18   ”   . . . can be barred or allowed at the tournament direc-
                    tor's discretion
6   ”   . . . must be barred from tournament play
——
61 conventions —total

I won't swear to the accuracy of this tabulation; a variation of a convention might be counted as a convention itself. But no matter how you figure it, with sixty-one gadgets you can open up your own hardware store.

Thus, when you play tournament bridge, you may run up against as many as fifty-five different conventions. (The Bridge League has considerately outlawed six of the most obtuse gadgets, but may change its mind next year.) You need a reliable bridge encyclopedia and perhaps a Ph.D. to be sure what the opponents are up to. Fortunately you needn't learn all the weird ones; the eager practitioners of these concoctions will get themselves in trouble often enough to more than offset your ignorance of how they do it.

Let's take a good look at a couple of these bidding gadgets. One is called the Texas Convention. Its ostensible purpose is to make the opening no-trump bidder the declarer at a major-suit game when *his partner* holds the suit. The theory is that the opening lead now comes up to—not through—the high-card combinations of the notrump hand, making the partnership less vulnerable to attack. Furthermore, the stronger hand is concealed, giving less information to the defenders.

Over partner's opening notrump, the responder bids four in the suit below his major suit, and opener must bid the next-higher suit. If responder thinks there is a game at hearts, the sequence is:

OPENER	RESPONDER
1 NT	4 ♢
4 ♡	Pass

If responder wants a spade contract, the bidding goes:

OPENER	RESPONDER
1 NT	4 ♡
4 ♠	Pass

Simple enough, isn't it? And it should be foolproof. But let's take a closer look. The Texas Convention installs one partner as absolute captain and reduces the other to automaton. You must be completely certain of the proper final contract before you arbitrarily declare your judgment as superior to that of the combined partnership.

How often does your holding make you this confident after your partner has opened with one notrump? *Possibly* ten times out of two hundred. And on seven of these ten hands, I estimate, it makes no difference which hand is led through. I grant that in two of the remaining three cases something is probably gained by the lead coming around to the opening notrumper, but I am dead sure something is lost in the third case.

Remember, an alert defender can double the artificial four-diamond or four-heart response to indicate a lead. Even if there is no double, the opening leader has a negative inference to guide him.

So what have we? A tricky new gadget that has to be explained—sometimes laboriously—to one's opponents and then carefully remembered. For all that, it earns its keep only about two times in two hundred. And there is one more drawback, common to all gadgets: the omnipresent temptation to overuse it just as a child with a new toy.

You hold ♠ 10-5, ♡ K-Q-10-6-4-2, ◇ Q-5-3, ♣ K-6. Partner bids a notrump, and you are playing the Texas Convention.

When you hear partner's notrump bid, you bristle and tingle and various glands begin to secrete, or whatever it is glands do. You bid four diamonds because you have to use your toy, and thus force partner to become declarer at four hearts. It is quite possible that four hearts is the best contract on the hand, but were you not tempted by your shiny new gadget, you would simply bid three hearts over one notrump. This is a forcing bid, and partner would respond either three notrump or four hearts. If he elected to bid three notrump, chances are this would be a superior and safer contract than four hearts. If you were not blinded by your gadget, you would at least give him a choice.

Another new gadget, the Roman variation of the Blackwood Convention, has already attracted quite a following, and I must confess a morbid fascination with it. It reads in part:

"Over a conventional Blackwood four-notrump bid, the responses take on different meanings as follows:

"Five clubs shows no aces or three aces

"Five diamonds shows one ace or four aces

"Five hearts shows two aces, both red or both black, or both major or both minor

"Five spades shows two aces, different both in color and rank of suit

"The same responses are used for kings over the Blackwood five-notrump asking bid."

What's the big deal? Simply this: when you use Roman Blackwood holding one ace in your own hand and find partner with two, you can identify one of his aces if he responds five hearts; if he responds five spades, you know both for a certainty.

Edgar Kaplan (of Kaplan-Sheinwold and Company) has written: "It is pure laziness not to use this Roman improvement."

Lazy am I, Mr. K.? I learned this gimmick when I played on the American team in the 1958 International Championship. Both the Argentinians and Italians were using it, and it behooved me to know what was going on. I felt at the time that it was perfectly sound, and still do.

But I don't have to play it—and it is a matter of principle, not laziness, that I don't. Roman Blackwood is just another artificial bid in the already cluttered bridge landscape, another set of tables and rules for the harassed bridge player to memorize (and occasionally forget that he has memorized).

The convention is both cute and catchy—and that is exactly what makes me uncomfortable. All this business about majors and minors, red and black. Who's kidding who? Why not come right out and say that a five-heart bid shows the aces of 1) spades and hearts or 2) spades and clubs or 3) hearts and diamonds or 4) diamonds and clubs. This is right to the point and would take no longer to explain to a new partner or inquisitive opponents. Why shilly-shally around with major-minor and red-black? But perhaps that is what makes this gimmick so appealing.

Both *black* aces, indeed! This is just doubletalk. A blind man using Braille cards is disenfranchised from using the convention. And what about the decks of cards with the pips printed in orange and green? A number of them are still being manufactured today. Or those with the pips of the four suits printed in four different colors? I get nightmares thinking that a color chart will be required equipment for tomorrow's bridge game. Think of the tragedy of the up-and-coming player who keeps getting to the wrong slams and never realizes that he is color blind.

If this be progress, I'll go it one better. The kings, besides being major or minor and red and black, are invariably one-eyed or two-eyed. I'll bet we can work that in somewhere! Offhand, I'm not sure which kings are two-eyed and which are right profile, but I'm darn well going to find out before Mr. K. calls me lazy again.

Blackwood is overused anyway (see Chapter 12), and now with the Roman variation, players will be stumbling over each other to get first crack at four notrump.

The bridge writers who are concocting the systems and inventing the gadgets have been called New Scientists by some. (Whether this appellation is a sincere tribute to genius or is slightly tinged with sarcasm I leave to the reader to decide.) These writers are trying to make an exact mathematical science out of a game that does not lend itself to it. Their rigid methods do not allow for human failure—or for that matter, for human brilliance, either. They try to make the perfect bid in all cases and never compromise for safety. Practically all bids are forcing to the New Scientists; only sissies jump the bidding to insure reaching game. Because of their methods and theories, the New Scientists are fit to be good partners only with their own ilk. With lesser players or with good but unfamiliar players as partners, their methods just cannot work.

I advise you to keep your bidding simple and natural, so you can have time to think out the problems you encounter. If you use good judgment, you will be a winning player. Clutter up your mind with gadgets, and you'll spend all your time trying to remember them—and wondering if your partner remembers them. Now back to the business at hand.

♠ ♥ 5 ♦ ♣
Responding Hand

A certain response to an opening bid has come back into fashion in recent years. It is the *pass.* But for the longest time it was considered almost effeminate to pass out partner's opening suit bid.

Many players seemed to bid out of a neurotic fear that they would miss game; after all, partner's opening one-bid might be just under two-bid stature. Yet these same players would make an equally shaky response on the ground that the *opponents* might have a game and a pass would make it easier for them to get there!

Therein lies the chief fallacy in responding on a very weak hand; on one and the same hand, you cannot logically fear both that your side has missed a game and that the opponents have a game. If *either* is a possibility, then neither is very likely.

If you hold a hand of only vague promise, and pass out your partner's one-bid, your side might miss a game, but most likely it would have been a lucky game. Those who try to bid every single possible game land in game on innumerable hands that can make only a part-score. Even when they stop short of game, they may find themselves in *too high* a part-score. Keep-the-bidding-open-on-a-prayer tactics produce a substantial net loss in the long run.

I don't want to inhibit you from taking reasonable risks, however. With a known and trusted partner you can loosen up a bit. But don't keep the bidding open if both your raise and your partner are doubtful; he may need no further encouragement to find an impossible game contract. And it is ironic how many overbidders play their dummies poorly.

Of course, apologize to a new partner if game was made after you passed out his opening bid; you must maintain partnership harmony at all costs. But content yourself with the realization that your tactics will win for you in the long run.

The vulnerability should influence your action. When non-vulnerable against vulnerable opponents, you can respond on weaker hands in order to interfere with the enemy. But don't delude yourself; you may be trying to stop nothing more than a part-score, if that. Don't look for sacrifices against nonexistent games.

Knowledge of partner's bidding tendencies is most helpful. If he is a notorious underbidder, you have to whisper some encouragement on mediocre holdings. If he "bids up his cards," don't bid up yours.

When you see a reasonable trump fit, you can step out more, but it is sheer lunacy to bid on junk just because you are looking for a better spot. Some examples:

1. ♠ 8 6 4   ♡ Q 7 3 2   ◊ J 5 4   ♣ 8 6 2
Partner opens one spade.
Pass. This is obvious, no matter who is vulnerable.

2. ♠ 8 6 4 2   ♡ 10 7 3 2   ◊ J 4 2   ♣ Q 2
Partner opens one club (or one diamond).
Pass. Even gunpoint shouldn't persuade you to try one of the majors, regardless of vulnerability. But if only the opponents were vulnerable and the opening bid—from a *safe and sane* partner—were one spade, you would raise to two spades for defensive reasons.

3. ♠ 4   ♡ 8 5 2   ◊ K J 10 8 4 3   ♣ 10 4 2
Partner opens one spade.
Pass, regardless of vulnerability. This is high-level stuff. Although the diamond suit is sound, you haven't nearly enough over-all strength to bid two diamonds, which is a one-round force on your partner. A one-notrump response would be a distortion because you have two suits completely unstopped, a singleton in partner's suit, and very few high cards. The singleton is the danger sign. It is dangerous to move even with far better hands if they contain a singleton or void in partner's suit. So the pass is clearly indicated. Now you have put partner on guard. If the opponents reopen the bidding, you can compete with your nice diamond suit, unmolested by unwanted rebids or unwarranted rescues by partner. Your first pass has told him the story.

WEAKNESS RESPONSES

Two responses plainly announce fairly weak hands: one notrump and a simple raise to two in partner's suit. Both are distinctly limited, and opener cannot expect too much. Some players call them "chance-giving" responses.

The minimum for a one-notrump response is 5 or 6 points. A raise to two in partner's suit can be made on fewer points if the hand contains four trumps and a doubleton. Three cards to a jack is just about the minimum

29

trump support for a raise; partner may have opened a 4-card suit. Only very rarely, when stuck for a bid, do I raise on 10-x-x or three small cards.

THE ONE-OVER-ONE RESPONSE

A response at the one-level in a new suit is frequently a minimum or shaded one. But this bid can also be made on a very strong hand, since it is an absolutely forcing bid unless made by a passed player. Later bidding reveals whether responder holds a weak or strong hand.

It is almost axiomatic that you should respond with one of any fairly respectable suit of your own in preference to one notrump.

THE TWO-OVER-ONE RESPONSE

The non-jump response of a new suit at the two-level (two-over-one) shows definite values, unlike the other responses just mentioned. It compels partner to rebid at the two- or three-level, since any new-suit response is a one-round force. This is not a response to be made on a whim or hope. For example:

1. ♠ 5   ♡ K 8 4 3   ◇ 10 6 2   ♣ A Q 8 5 3
Partner opens one spade.
Bid one notrump, not two clubs. This hand is just not good enough to force partner to the two-level.

2. ♠ A Q 8 5 3   ♡ K 8 4 3   ◇ 10 6 2   ♣ 5
This is the same hand with spades and clubs reversed. Partner opens one club (or one diamond).
Bid one spade; it does not raise the bidding level.

The two-over-one response should always show at least a fair hand—say a minimum of 10 high-card points. It can show a great deal more. Players frequently use it as a temporizing bid, for hands near the slam zone, rather than crowd the bidding with an immediate jump. More on this anon.

MAJOR-SUIT DOUBLE RAISE

Most players use this bid as a force to game unless made by a passed hand. A modern tendency, approved here, is to permit a dead minimum opening to pass. In any event, the bid has definite limits. Look for a better first response on any hand with slam possibilities.

MAJOR-SUIT TRIPLE RAISE

The raise from one to four in partner's major suit is a specialized bid, more pre-emptive and with less high-card strength than the double raise. But it is definitely not bereft of high-card values. Usually it indicates one less high-card trick than the double raise, but compensates with one more playing trick.
For example:

1. ♠ A Q 4 3   ♡ K 5   ◇ 7 4   ♣ K J 9 3 2
Partner bids one spade.
Bid three spades. 13 high-card points and fine trump support.

Now change to:

2. ♠ Q 6 4 3 2   ♡ K 5   ◇ 4   ♣ K J 9 3 2
Partner again bids one spade.
Bid four spades. This is a typical triple raise with fewer high cards but more distributional values.

The meaning of these two raises is different when made by a passed hand. Since partner then has the privilege of passing a raise to three, your raise to four logically states that you insist upon game—therefore, you have a better hand. If partner has distinct additional values, he should move toward slam after a triple raise, since it shows just under opening-bid values.

MINOR-SUIT RAISES

Over partner's one-club or one-diamond opener you can usually find some economical temporizing bid at the one-level if you want to make sure of reaching game. Thus the immediate raise from one to three in a minor is rather vague. My feeling is that it should signify a fairly strong game invitation but not be an absolute force.

♠ A 5   ♡ K 4   ◇ K 10 6 3 2   ♣ 9 7 3 2
Partner opens one diamond.
Bid three diamonds. This is your best shot. If partner passes with a dead minimum, you are not chagrined. If he bids three notrump, he should have a decent play for it. If your hand were a bit stronger, you would look for a better bid than three diamonds.

Minor-suit single raises always show at least four trumps and deny a good biddable major-suit holding. Their overall strength is about the same as a major-suit single raise.

JUMP RESPONSES IN NOTRUMP

A two-notrump response to an opening suit bid of one is based on pure point-count calculation; you need 13 to 15 high-card points in a balanced hand with stoppers in the three unbid suits. If you want to maintain partnership harmony, don't shade this bid.

There is no need to stretch to find a two-notrump response. Some exploration may uncover a major-suit fit, and this often proves a safer game contract. You can always try notrump later, after you have concluded there is no major-suit game. A sensible bridge player resents the partner who is a notrump hog and always manages to come up with a thundering two notrump in response to any opening bid of one in a suit. Often he goes down when four of a major was cold.

The immediate jump to three notrump over partner's suit opening is a rigid bid. It indicates 16 or 17 points with 4-3-3-3 distribution (occasionally with 4-4-3-2). Don't broaden the use of this bid. With so much strength you are close to the slam zone, and you don't want to give up the chance for a good suit slam.

THE JUMP SHIFT

A jump in a new suit shows definite interest in slam, and so it is covered in Chapter 11, Slam Bidding. Suffice it to say here that it is an absolute force to game and there is no ceiling for this bid.

CHOICE OF RESPONSES

There is no substitute for common sense and experience when faced with a choice of responses. However, I can make a few generalizations.

A raise in partner's suit tends to be more encouraging than a one-notrump response. Normally a holding of four trumps suggests the raise. However, a notrump response may work out better on a hand with four trumps if it contains no distributional advantage and a minimum of high cards.

A frequent problem is whether to raise partner or show your suit on a hand of intermediate strength. The following three examples summarize this situation very nicely:

1. ♠ K Q 8 5   ♡ 10 6 4   ◇ K 10   ♣ A J 10 3
Partner bids one spade.
Bid three spades. Always prefer the double raise if you have four good trumps and your hand otherwise qualifies. There is no point to showing the clubs.

2. ♠ Q J 5   ♡ 10 6 2   ◇ 8 4   ♣ A Q 8 4 2
Partner bids one spade.
Bid two spades. The limited strength make this a "one-bid hand." You cannot show both your club suit and your spade support, and it is more important to indicate the major-suit fit.

3. ♠ K J 5   ♡ 9 4 2   ◇ 8 3   ♣ A K 6 3 2
Partner bids one spade.
Bid two clubs. Now your hand is good enough for you to bid clubs first and then raise spades. Moreover, an immediate jump to three spades is not advisable with only three trumps.

TWO-SUITERS

Your objective in responding with a two-suiter is to get your message over economically and sensibly. If you are strong enough to show both suits regardless of partner's rebid, then you paint the most accurate picture possible by bidding them in normal order—the higher-ranking first if they are equal in length, and the longer suit first if they are unequal. With lesser strength you must guard against getting up too high too fast and this may require you to distort the relative length of your suits.

1. ♠ K J 10 5   ♡ 4 3   ◇ J 8   ♣ A K 10 4 2
Partner opens one diamond.
Bid two clubs. The outlook for game is bright, and you want to indicate your distribution accurately by bidding both suits in normal sequence. Economy is also served by bidding clubs first. If you respond one spade and partner rebids two hearts, you have to go to the three-level to show your clubs.

2. ♠ K J 9 4   ♡ 6   ◇ J 8 5   ♣ A 9 6 5 3
Partner opens one heart.
Bid one spade. You are not good enough for a two-over-one response. Also, you want to explore the major-suit possibility at once, since you do not intend to make two voluntary bids.

3. ♠ K J 9 5   ♡ K J 9 7   ◇ 6 3   ♣ J 9 5

Partner bids one diamond.

Bid one heart. Here you choose the lower-ranking of two equal suits to guarantee finding a major-suit fit if there is one. If partner has hearts, he will raise.
If he has spades, he has room to show the suit at the one-level.

If you respond one spade, you may miss out on a possible heart fit. Partner
may have four fair hearts but too weak a hand to bid them at the two-level.
You are too weak to make a second bid unless forced, and you may easily land
at an inferior one-notrump or two-diamond contract.

4. ♠ K Q J 5   ♡ A Q 8 3   ◇ 7 5   ♣ 10 6 3

Partner bids one diamond.

Bid one spade. This hand is strong enough to warrant two bids, so you can
show your suits in normal order. No need to worry whether partner can bid
hearts, because you plan to bid them on your own.

Some corrosive responding habits have crept into use, and this is the
spot to discourage them to assure contented partnerships and winning
scores.

THE EXAGGERATED ONE-NOTRUMP RESPONSE TO ONE CLUB

Some players exaggerate a natural implication and make this bid with
12, 13, or even 14 points. They thereby miss more than their share of games
when they're playing with an unfamiliar partner.

It is logical enough that a one-notrump response to a one-club opening
should promise certain values, because it skips over three other possible
bids and gets you to the brink of the two-level. Surely with a skimpy 6-7
point chance-giving hand you would make a cheaper bid, even if you had
to manufacture a suit.

Thus you might have 8 to 10 points, possibly 11, for a one-notrump
response to one club. But no more. There is no sense in exaggerating this
logical bidding implication into a brand-new system. We have enough of
these already.

ALWAYS SHOW A 4-CARD MAJOR?

One school of players believes that you must *always* respond in a major
if you have a 4-card holding, no matter how weak. Their fervor in seeking
out the mystic 4-4 major-suit fit blinds them to the drawbacks of this pur-

suit. They may get to an occasional good major-suit game that mere mortals miss, but they also land in impossible part-score suit contracts where you and I would be wrapping up one notrump with an overtrick.

♠ J 8 6 3   ♡ 9 7 4   ◇ A 10 6   ♣ K J 5
Partner opens one heart.

Bid one notrump. There is no reason to show the anemic spades. A notrump response shows the general pattern and strength of the hand. If the hand belongs in spades, partner can bid the suit. Of course, you may miss out if partner *should* have opened one spade, but you cannot base your bids on a presumption of an error by partner.

FREE RAISES AND BIDS

The significance of the free raise is greatly exaggerated by many players. If you have a bad hand, an overcall of partner's opener gets you off the hook, and you pass gratefully; but if you have a sound raise, the overcall shouldn't deter you and partner shouldn't expect real power.

1. ♠ K 8 4 2   ♡ 6 3   ◇ J 10 3 2   ♣ 7 3 2
Partner opens one spade.

With no overcall: *Bid two spades.* After an overcall: *Pass;* if partner is very strong, he will have another chance to speak. However, if your hand were a shade better—the diamond king instead of the J-10, for example—you would raise to two spades despite the overcall.

The same thinking applies to bidding your own suit at the one-level.

2. ♠ Q 10 8 3 2   ♡ 7 5 3   ◇ K J 4   ♣ 9 3
Partner opens one club; next player overcalls one heart.

Bid one spade. There is no reason to be pre-empted out of your convenient bit by a measly one-heart overcall. What better time to show your spades than at the one-level? Besides, the suit is not strong enough to back in later.

A bid in a new suit is still a one-round force, so don't stretch unduly to find a free bid. For example, if the spade suit in the last hand were J-8-6-4-3, you should pass.

The Opener Rebids

An opening bid of one in a suit is hardly precise; it can be made on 12 high-card points or double that. It is the opener's *rebid* that narrows down the range. It should describe his hand as 1) a minimum or near-minimum opener, or 2) a maximum or near-maximum, or, at least, 3) something in between.

It is axiomatic that although you can bid only your own hand, you are nonetheless bidding for the partnership. Thus the action opener takes should be influenced by partner's response.

AFTER A ONE-NOTRUMP RESPONSE

This limiting response places partner with no more than 10 points and possibly as little as 5 or 6. With a balanced hand, you need more than 16 points for game; if you have less, pass like a little man and be happy with your part-score. You should have good reason for bidding over one notrump —more than 16 points in high cards or some distributional advantage; otherwise you are just jeopardizing your part-score and getting higher in a hopeless cause.

But what exactly is a balanced hand? In my view it is one that has neither a singleton in any suit nor worthless doubletons in two suits. This may seem rather broad, and it is intentionally so.

Some minor defect for notrump play is not reason enough for you to rebid. Nor is the mere presence of a rebiddable suit or a second biddable suit.

Now for some examples:

1. ♠ Q 5 4   ♡ A K 9 8 7   ◇ K J 3   ♣ 4 2
2. ♠ A 5 2   ♡ K Q 10 4   ◇ K Q J 3   ♣ 7 6
3. ♠ J 5   ♡ K Q 10 7 4   ◇ 8 6 2   ♣ A Q 5

In each case you opened one heart and partner replies one notrump.
Pass all three hands—and fast. In Hands 1 and 3, the fact that hearts are rebiddable is of minor importance. You have gone far enough, and the off-chance that the hand might play better in hearts is not reason to increase the level of the contract. Similarly, in Hand 2 there is no reason to show the diamond suit. Note that all three hands count to less than 16 points.

However, a worthless singleton *is* a good reason to look for a better spot. Sometimes you have to rebid over one notrump on a minimum hand simply because you can't stand to play at notrump. On these two hands, you open one heart and partner responds one notrump:

1. ♠ 5   ♡ K Q J 6 4   ◊ 10 8 7 6   ♣ A K J
Rebid two hearts. The spade suit is too dangerous, particularly since partner passed up a chance to bid it.

2. ♠ 7 4   ♡ A Q 10 6 3   ◊ A J 7 4 2   ♣ 3
Bid two diamonds to show your second suit.

In Hand 2, note that a two-diamond bid is the only sensible action even with this minimum opener. This clearly disproves the mistaken notion of many bridge players that such a change of suit indicates a strong hand. All the second bid shows is a distributional hand and a distaste for notrump; it implies no extra values. Opener has committed the partnership only to the two-level; responder is free to pass or to return to two hearts.

If opener's rebid is in a higher-ranking suit than his first bid, responder can logically infer a stronger hand, since he will now have to go to the three-level to indicate preference for the first suit. But if opener has bid his suits in "normal" order, responder must be modest in his aspirations.

That's why, if you have a potential game-going hand, you should step out with it. Don't be bashful about jumping in your second suit.

3. ♠ A K 10 7 5   ♡ A Q J 6 2   ◊ K J   ♣ 5
You open one spade; partner bids one notrump.
Bid three hearts. Partner should have some sort of fit in one of the majors, giving you a good play for game. After all, he didn't pass out your opening bid. Such a jump may get you overboard occasionally, but you miss a game far oftener by making the minimum non-forcing two-heart rebid instead.

The same considerations apply to a one-suit hand:

4. ♠ A K J 7 5 4   ♡ J 4   ◊ A 8 3   ♣ K 3
You open one spade; partner bids one notrump.

Rebid three spades. A jump bid in the same suit over a one-notrump response is not forcing, only invitational. If partner accepts the offer, there should be a good play for game—at either spades or notrump. If he passes three spades, you are high enough. A simple two-spade rebid would be cowardly; you'd make that call without the ace of diamonds.

A raise to two notrump or three notrump is a simple point-count calculation on a balanced hand:

5. ♠ K 5   ♡ K Q J 9 6   ◇ A J 9 3   ♣ K J
You open one heart; partner bids one notrump.
Bid two notrump. This is a compromise bid. Two diamonds would be inadequate, and you are not good enough to jump in diamonds or hearts. Two notrump advertises a hand considerably over a minimum and requests partner to go on to game if he has something over a minimum one-notrump response.

AFTER A SINGLE RAISE

Remember, the single raise discovers a suit fit but also announces a limited hand. There is no point in looking for a better spot; unless you see a chance for game, pass without a qualm. This means passing many a hand that is considerably over an opening bid. For example:

1. ♠ A K Q 7 5   ♡ 3 2   ◇ K Q 4   ♣ Q 10 4
2. ♠ A K 8 6 2   ♡ J 3   ◇ K Q J 5   ♣ 10 4
On both hands you open one spade; partner raises to two spades.
Pass, in both cases. Sure, you have convenient rebids available—three spades on Hand 1, and three diamonds on Hand 2. But a further bid can easily get you too high. You might not make even three spades. The chance for game is not sufficient to justify this risk.

KNOW THY PARTNER

Naturally, in all close situations be guided by your knowledge of your partner. In the last two examples you'd pass with *almost* any partner. With Caspar Milquetoast you'd make another effort.

Don't forget the opponents. If their defense is sloppy, it is almost criminal not to take some small liberties at their expense.

Now for some better hands:

1. ♠ A Q 9 7 4 3   ♡ A Q J   ◇ Q 4   ♣ 9 4
You bid one spade; partner raises to two spades.

Rebid three spades. The distribution makes a try at game distinctly worth-while. The hand is worth just three spades, which gives partner the option of passing if he had a minimum raise. Only a very timid partner would make you even think of going directly to four. Opposite a wild overbidder, you might toy with the idea of passing to two.

2. ♠ A Q J 6 5   ♡ 3   ◇ A J 7 4   ♣ K 9 2

You bid one spade; partner raises to two spades.

Bid three diamonds—if you have a very discerning partner. You're aiming at game, a distinct possibility with your high-card strength and distribution. If partner had a maximum spade raise and has help in diamonds, he will bid four spades. If he bids only three spades, you pass. This is the super-scientific approach. *But rebid three spades*—if you have an average partner, neither underbidder nor overbidder. This at least has the merit of not aiding the defense.

AFTER A DOUBLE RAISE

A double raise in a major commits you to game. The only remaining questions are: 1) Is there a slam? and 2) Is three notrump a better contract?

The first question is discussed in Chapter 11 on Slam Bidding. The answer to the second question is almost always No. Partner is practically sure to have four cards in your major suit for his raise. Even if both hands are balanced, there is probably a weak doubleton somewhere or a weak combined suit, and the odds are better than five to one that the hand will play better in a suit contract.

A double raise in a minor is a different kettle of fish; it is just a fairly strong game invitation (see page 31). If you have two or three suits stopped and full values for the opener, hazard a three-notrump reply. If you have an unbalanced hand and concrete extra values, go after a minor-suit game. If you hold a good 4-card major suit, show it over partner's jump and perhaps he'll be able to bid three notrump. But you may pass with a dead minimum.

AFTER A ONE-OVER-ONE RESPONSE

The one-notrump rebid is a useful catch-all. It warns of a balanced minimum hand, but does not guarantee sure stoppers in all unbid suits. Since you opened the bidding, you must put on the brakes with this rebid so you don't unduly encourage partner on a minimum hand. You open one diamond; partner bids one heart (in each of the following hands):

1. ♠ 8 7 4   ♡ Q 3   ◇ A Q 10 4   ♣ A Q 5 3

Rebid one notrump. Partner's one-heart response is forcing, and you have a minimum balanced hand. True, you have no spade stopper, but you can't have everything. A club rebid would promise more of a two-suiter. You don't want to excite partner with this meager holding, and you'll be happy if he permits you to play at one notrump.

2. ♠ J 4   ♡ A 5   ◇ K Q 7 6 3   ♣ Q J 10 8

Rebid one notrump. The 5-4-2-2 distribution is not too unbalanced, and you want to warn partner that your hand is minimum. Again, you have no spade stopper, but you haven't promised one. Two clubs, although not a strong bid, would imply more than a dead minimum such as this.

3. ♠ J 5 3   ♡ A J 4   ◇ K Q 10 3   ♣ K 10 3

Rebid one notrump. Repress the urge to raise hearts. Your hand is completely balanced, with something in every suit, and is pretty close to a minimum opening.

4. ♠ A J 3   ♡ J 5   ◇ K Q J 6 2   ♣ K 5 2

Rebid one notrump. This is more descriptive than two diamonds, and you have hardly enough over a minimum to get excited.

In respectable bridge-playing circles, a minor-suit rebid shows five and three-quarter cards! I enjoy stating this concept because of the startled looks that usually result. What I mean is that three times out of four the bid shows a 6-card holding. With only five cards there is usually a more pertinent bid available, as in Hand 4.

5. ♠ A 4   ♡ 8 6   ◇ K Q J 6 3 2   ♣ K 6 2

Rebid two diamonds. This is a darn good 6-card suit. Although the other two suits are stopped, you like the hand too much to simply rebid one notrump and undersell your diamonds.

CAUTION: Don't wait for a 6-card suit before rebidding a major. Game in a major occurs about three times oftener than game in a minor, so a *good* 5-card major virtually cries out to be rebid.

6. ♠ K 8 3   ♡ K 10 9   ◇ A K J 10 7   ♣ A J

Rebid two notrump, a strong game urge requiring 18-19 points and stoppers in all unbid suits. This one clearly fills the bill, with 19 full points plus two tens and a dandy 5-card suit to boot. With only three trumps, a jump in hearts would be misleading.

7. ♠ A 10 9   ♡ Q 10 4   ◇ A K Q 7 2   ♣ A J

Rebid three notrump. This hand counts 20 high-card points and appears to have seven taking tricks on top plus potential double stoppers in the unbid black suits. Any lesser bid would expect too much of even a confirmed over-bidder.

8. ♠ A 10 6 5   ♡ 10 4   ♢ A K 7 3   ♣ Q J 2
Rebid one spade. You should be delighted to show a respectable 4-card major suit at the one-level whenever the opportunity arises. Partner may have four spades headed by a queen or jack, and might never be able to bid them on his own. If you don't seize this chance to try out the suit, you may miss your only sound game bet. Avoid the one-notrump rebid here, even though you have a balanced minimum with the adverse suits stopped. If notrump is the best spot, you'll have a chance to get there later.

9. ♠ 8 7 6 5   ♡ Q 10   ♢ A K 7 3   ♣ A J 9
Rebid one notrump. These spades aren't a suit; they're an eyesore. Let partner bid the suit if he has it.

10. ♠ 6 5   ♡ 9 3   ♢ K Q J 7 5   ♣ A K 10 6
Rebid two clubs. This tells partner your strength is massed in the minors. He can still try notrump or let you play in one of your suits.

11. ♠ K 2   ♡ J 3   ♢ K Q 9 7 6   ♣ A Q 6 3
Rebid one notrump. Identical distribution as Hand 10 except you have a spade stopper and your club suit is shabbier. It is a bit over a minimum, but not enough so that this call will keep you out of a reasonable game contract.

RAISING PARTNER'S SUIT

I enthusiastically prescribe a raise in partner's suit whenever it helps solve future bidding problems. The raise has a salutary effect on partner. And it doesn't require terrific trump support; any 4-card holding will do, even a good 3-carder. However, adapt to your partner as always. Nothing seems to unnerve a near-beginner so much as having to play a suit contract with a 4-3 trump holding. So be careful—the weaker your partner, the better your trump support should be.

In the previous examples you haven't really been tempted to support partner's suit. Now we'll survey this subject. You open one diamond; partner bids one heart (in each of the following hands):

1. ♠ Q 10 5   ♡ 10 9 6 2   ♢ A K Q 4   ♣ Q 5
Bid two hearts. No need to put on the brakes with a one-notrump rebid. This hand was a minimum opener, but partner's heart bid has improved it.

2. ♠ A K   ♡ 8 6 4 2   ◇ K 10 8 5 3 2   ♣ 7

Bid two hearts. This is clear-cut. Why mess with the diamonds when you have found a major-suit fit?

3. ♠ 6 2   ♡ A J 3   ◇ K Q J 6 4   ♣ K 10 6

Bid two hearts. Support the major in preference to rebidding your minor. Three cards including two honors are more than adequate trump support.

4. ♠ K 8 6 2   ♡ A Q 5   ◇ K J 6 4 2   ♣ 3

Bid two hearts. This requires discipline, because you'd like to show the spades and probe for a 4-4 fit there. But your hand is not robust enough to both bid spades and then support hearts, and so you settle for the heart raise.

5. ♠ K 10 7 4   ♡ A Q 10   ◇ K Q 5 3 2   ♣ 3

Bid one spade. Now you do have enough to bid spades and then support hearts. Moreover, a simple raise to two hearts would be an underbid and a double raise with only three trumps should be avoided. So one spade is a wise compromise.

6. ♠ 8   ♡ A 7 6 3   ◇ A Q 8 6 2   ♣ K Q 3

Bid three hearts. 15 high-card points, 4-card trump support, and the distributional advantages make game a reasonable hope. This bid is not forcing, so partner can get out if he has a bad hand.

7. ♠ A 6 3 2   ♡ K J 7 3   ◇ A Q J 6   ♣ 4

Bid three hearts. Don't go spade hunting with a good 4-card heart support and the values for a jump bid. Should partner show slam interest, you have a little something in reserve and would be happy to bid spades then to show the ace.

8. ♠ 3   ♡ K 10 4   ◇ A J 10 6 3   ♣ A Q 10 4

Bid two clubs. Another compromise. Two hearts doesn't do the hand justice, and a jump in hearts requires a fourth trump. Although two clubs is not forcing, partner will probably find another bid if his hand would help produce game, and you will then support hearts.

9. ♠ A K 3   ♡ K Q 6 5   ◇ A J 9 5 2   ♣ 3

Bid four hearts. Game must be worth a try, so don't pass the buck to partner with a non-forcing three-heart bid and risk his passing it out.

Note that this four-heart bid is logically a bigger bid than three hearts. Don't confuse it with the triple raise in *response* to an opening bid, which has a partial pre-emptive motive. There would be no need to pre-empt in Hand 9, because the opponents have stayed quiet for a full round of bidding.

10. ♠ A 10 9 5   ♡ K Q 9 3   ◇ A K J 10 3   ♣ None

Bid two spades. You should really be gunning for slam and therefore need a bigger bid than in Hand 9. Fortunately, there is an ascending scale of bids for opener in raising partner's suit: first the simple raise, next the double raise, then the raise to game, and finally a jump in a new suit. The last of these is absolutely forcing to game.

11. ♠ 3   ♡ A K 4 2   ◇ K Q J 7 2   ♣ A K 2

Bid three clubs. Another slam candidate. This time you jump in a 3-card suit, which will suggest spade shortness later when you strongly support hearts. If partner gets enthusiastic about clubs, you return to hearts at the same level of bidding.

KNOW THY PARTNER

With a partner who may not recognize a forcing situation or a plain weak sister, four hearts is the better bid on Hands 10 and 11. It is an underbid, of course, and you may miss slam. But if partner passes out your rebid ("Oh, was it forcing?"), a sure game will have been scuttled.

12. ♠ 4   ♡ K 5   ◇ A K J 10 3   ♣ A K J 9 7

Bid three clubs. This forcing rebid is based on overall power rather than strong heart support. Game may be in hearts if partner rebids the suit; in notrump if he bids spades; or it may be in one of the minors. In any event, you want a fling at it.

AFTER A TWO-OVER-ONE RESPONSE

Rebidding after a two-over-one response is usually easier than after a one-over-one response. Partner has advertised definite values, and taken on a certain responsibility. In rebidding you often have to rely on the security provided by his bid, almost as you would lean on a crutch. Four times out of five he will find a second bid no matter what you do.

In general, you should try to make a natural rebid. However, the greater stability of the bidding structure dictates some adjustments:

1. ♠ K J 5   ♡ A Q 10 4   ◇ K J 6 5   ♣ 8 2

You open one heart; partner bids two clubs.

Bid two notrump. In the old days a two-notrump bid showed quite a good hand—say, at least 15 or 16 points—and so you would have had to rebid two diamonds on this 14-pointer, a bid that implies better distribution and more or less denies spade stoppers. But modern bridge theory has changed all this. The two-club bid promises a good hand and you can now make the far more descriptive notrump rebid without fear. Partner has no right to play you for anything much over a minimum.

2. ♠ A 10 9 8 2   ♡ 9 3   ◇ A Q 8 4   ♣ Q 3
You open one spade; partner bids two clubs.
Bid two diamonds. You are forced to bid, and this is the most descriptive bid available. Also, it saves you from repeating your not-too-potent spade suit. Partner should not assume you have any additional values for this bid.

3. ♠ A 10 9 8 2   ♡ 9 3   ◇ Q 3   ♣ A Q 8 4
You open one spade; partner bids two diamonds.
Bid two spades. This is identical to Hand 2 except that the minor suits have been transposed. Here you rebid spades, because it is the cheapest response to describe this minimum hand. You cannot go to the three-level to show the second suit, because this would imply a far stronger hand.

4. ♠ A Q 6 5 4   ♡ 8 3 2   ◇ K Q 3   ♣ Q 5
You open one spade; partner bids two diamonds.
Bid two spades. A raise to three diamonds would bespeak more playing strength and would probably evoke a three-notrump bid from partner on almost any hand. You cannot afford such gymnastics on this mediocre assortment, so bid two spades even though you are not proud of your spade suit.

5. ♠ A K 8 6 3   ♡ 8 3 2   ◇ A Q 3   ♣ Q 5
You open one spade; partner bids two diamonds.
Bid three diamonds. With 2 points more than in Hand 4, you should be delighted to show off a little muscle by raising to the three-level. Partner is more likely to carry on over this bid than over the tame-sounding two spades. If spades is the proper spot, partner will get you there.

6. ♠ A Q 8 5 4   ♡ K Q 3   ◇ Q J 9   ♣ 9 2
You open one spade; partner bids two hearts.
Bid three hearts. The odds are that a two-level major-suit response is based on a 5-card holding, and it behooves you to raise at the slightest provocation. Your bid merely confirms the fit; it announces nothing much over your opener.

AFTER A JUMP SHIFT

The watchword after a jump response in a new suit is naturalness. Partner has taken on full responsibility for the eventual game or slam contract, and is pleading with you to show exactly what you have. He should not play you for additional values because you now raise his suit or show a new suit—*whether higher-ranking or not.* The level of your bid, however, carries certain implications. For example, if you opened with one heart, partner responded with three diamonds, and you now bid four clubs, it must mean you are willing to play for an eleven-trick game. But if your rebid is three spades, it promises nothing extra in high cards—merely a holding of five hearts and four spades.

AFTER A JUMP RESPONSE IN NOTRUMP

The same general theory holds true after a two-notrump response by partner. If you bid a second suit at the three-level, it merely warns against notrump and suggests an alternate contract. Partner should not take it into his head that you are looking for slam; if you have the tickets and are slam probing, you'll tell him about it on the next round.

Thus, the bidding sequence one heart—two notrump—three hearts suggests only that opener has a good heart suit and thinks three notrump may not be the best eventual contract. The heart rebid should not be construed as either a slam try *or a sign-off*. The same reasoning applies if opener bids a new suit—either higher- or lower-ranking—after two notrump.

If partner responds three notrump to your opener, picture a 4-3-3-3 hand with 16 or 17 points, and you should then find it simple to decide whether to pass or go after slam.

KNOW THY PARTNER

Beware the happy type of notrump hog who responds two notrump on 11 or 12 points. He is the same character who feels impelled to bid three notrump when blessed with 14 or 15. Leave him in his favorite contract unless you have a good many surplus points or the equivalent in distributional advantage.

What do you do when you open a psychic and partner jumps? Elementary: don't open psychics with strangers in the first place. If you must bid psychics, save them for your favorite and most tolerant partner. He can wrestle with your genius. I absolve myself from responsibility.

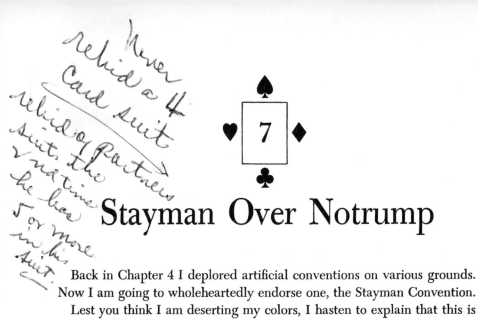

rebid Never Card a 4 suit
rebid a suit of Partner
2nd time he has 5 or more in his suit

♠ ♥ 7 ♦ ♣

Stayman Over Notrump

Back in Chapter 4 I deplored artificial conventions on various grounds. Now I am going to wholeheartedly endorse one, the Stayman Convention.

Lest you think I am deserting my colors, I hasten to explain that this is more than a gadget. It is named, not unreasonably, after one man, Samuel Stayman. But during the time he was experimenting with it so successfully, hundreds of other bridge players were simultaneously working along similar lines, and many had already been using the Stayman principle in a natural way.

The Stayman Convention was not artificially contrived; it grew out of a natural situation. After an opening one-notrump bid responder bid two (or three) clubs to show a genuine club suit. (Many players considered two a forcing bid; others played a jump response to *three* as their forcing bid.) Either way opener would tend to show any decent 4-card suit he happened to hold. From this evolved the Stayman Convention, an artificial response of two clubs to an opening bid of one notrump. It is a forcing bid and inquires whether opener has a 4-card major suit of Q-x-x-x or better.

The Stayman Convention rests on two conclusions:

1) Because opener's one-notrump bid has told almost his whole story, partner, whose hand is unknown, should take the initiative in placing the final contract.

2) Because a 4-4 major-suit fit usually plays better at a contract of four in the major than at three notrump, partner needs some method of probing for a 4-4 major-suit fit. For example:

WEST	EAST
♠ A J 6 3	♠ K 7 5 4
♡ K Q 5	♡ A 7 4
◇ K 7 3	◇ A 6 5 4 2
♣ K 8 3	♣ 5

Four spades is a romp if the opposing spades do not break too badly. But three notrump is beaten after a club opening unless the spade queen is onside.

Of course, you don't need convincing that a good 4-4 major-suit fit usually pays a handsome dividend. So let us consider how you find out if there is such a fit after an opening bid of one notrump. In the old days you couldn't. Partner may have, quite correctly, ignored a perfectly good 4- or 5-card suit to make the more comprehensive one-notrump call. Yet nobody dared respond to a notrump with a suit like K-7-5-4. And if a daring soul had, how would opener know whether the two-spade response showed a mangy 4-carder or a respectable 5-card suit?

If there was ambiguity about the suit strength shown by a major-suit response at the two-level, there was out-and-out disagreement about the over-all strength it should indicate. A third of the nation considered it a weakness sign-off; another third, a one-round forcing bid; and the rest just bid and prayed.

Stayman neatly solves the problem. The two-club response to an opening one-notrump bid became an artificial and forcing bid inquiring whether opener has a 4-card major suit of Q-x-x-x or better. Responder's bid promises nothing in the way of clubs, but does imply interest in the major suits.

Thus, responder no longer needs to bid a 4-card major; instead he asks partner to show his. It follows that if responder bids a suit, it must be at least five cards in length.

The Stayman two-club response is just one tool available to opener's partner. He is still free to invite game by bidding two notrump; to force to game by jumping to three of a suit, which lets partner pick the spot; or to jump directly to game or slam if the points or distribution add up.

Since the Stayman two-club bid is an absolute force on opener, it follows that a response of two in any other suit is clearly a weakness sign-off bid; opener is then required to pass unless he has both a maximum notrump and a particularly good fit in the suit named.

After the two-club bid, opener bids a 4-card major if he has one. (If he has both majors, he bids spades first and hopes for a chance to show hearts.) If he has no 4-card major, he bids two notrump to show a maximum opening notrump, or two diamonds to show less point count.*

---

*Many experts eliminate the two-notrump rebid; they require that opener bid two diamonds whenever he lacks a 4-card major, no matter what his point count. I recommend a middle course for casual partnerships; rebid two notrump only with a really maximum notrump; bid two diamonds on all hands up to 17-plus points.

Now responder is in the driver's seat. If a suit fit has been found, he raises the suit to invite game or he bids game himself, depending on his strength. If no fit has been unearthed, he returns to notrump—two notrump as a game invitation or three notrump if the point count warrants it.

Let's look at some example hands to see how and when to use Stayman. Partner opens with one notrump and next player passes in each case:

1. ♠ K 7 5 4   ♡ 10   ◊ A J 6 2   ♣ Q J 5 3
Bid two clubs. If partner rebids two spades, you jump to game in spades. Otherwise, you bid game in notrump.

2. ♠ 10 7 2   ♡ K 10 7 4 3   ◊ 6   ♣ 9 6 4 2
Bid two hearts. With your singleton, you certainly prefer hearts to notrump. Partner cannot misinterpret your bid. He knows you have a weak hand, and he will not raise without a good heart fit *and* a maximum point count.

3. ♠ 9 7 2   ♡ 10 4   ◊ K 10 5 4 2   ♣ 8 3 2
Pass. This, to be sure, is a weakness bid, just as two diamonds would be. But you don't bid two diamonds just because it cannot be misunderstood. This is still a balanced hand. Therefore, you have no reason to believe eight tricks can be made at diamonds, but not seven at notrump.

4. ♠ A 10 4 2   ♡ 10 7 3   ◊ Q 5 2   ♣ K Q 3
Bid three notrump. With this perfectly balanced hand there is no advantage in looking for a major-suit fit. You are not likely to produce an extra ruffing trick, and partner's bid also shows a balanced hand. So play for nine tricks rather than ten, even if partner has four spades.

5. ♠ Q J 6 5   ♡ 9 4 2   ◊ K 10 3   ♣ Q 10 5
Bid two notrump. Again, with the classic balanced hand you refrain from Stayman. With only 8 points, you merely invite a notrump game.

6. ♠ A 10 4 2   ♡ 8 7 3 2   ◊ Q 10   ♣ K Q 3
Bid three notrump. Even with a 4-4-3-2 pattern, there is no advantage in a major-suit probe if your strength is well distributed and your doubleton boasts some value. A two-club response might well steer the defense to the best opening lead, whereas they may easily open one of the majors when you *apparently* deny much major-suit strength by bidding three notrump.

7. ♠ K Q 10 8 5 4   ♡ A 4   ◊ 10 5   ♣ 9 7 2
Bid three spades. Partner will bid four with any three spades to an honor, or three notrump with a doubleton. Either way, it's all right with you and should land you in the right spot.

Please observe that the Stayman Convention was used in only two of the seven hands—once directly with a two-club response and once indirectly with a two-level suit response.

I venture that on half the occasions partner opens with one notrump the Stayman Convention comes into play either directly or indirectly. The seven sample hands were chosen to dramatize a point. Knowing when to use a convention distinguishes the pro from the plumber. Stayman has its special use, but that's all. You needn't be a slave to it and abandon all the other possible bids, such as a raise in notrump, a jump bid in a good suit, and, oh yes, the pass.

The Stayman Convention is really quite simple. However, it has several ramifications you should at least be familiar with:

SHOWING A WEAK CLUB HAND

Since the two-club response is artificial, this creates the problem of how to show a weak hand with a long club suit that belongs in some low part-score—such as six clubs to the queen-jack and no more than an outside queen. Some players respond two clubs at their first turn and three clubs next to show such a hand and demand that they be permitted to play at three clubs. Others bid three clubs immediately; they reserve the two-club—three-club sequence for other occasions when they want to find out what else opener has to say. I prefer the latter treatment.

SHOWING A 5-CARD MAJOR

There is certainly no point in showing a 4-card major after partner denies a 4-card holding in that suit. It follows that a voluntary bid at this stage must show a 5-card holding. For example:

NORTH	SOUTH
1 NT	2 ♣
2 ♡	2 ♠

Opener does not have four spades as good as Q-x-x-x, or he would have bid two spades first. Thus responder's two-spade bid shows five cards, and opener is expected to raise with Q-x-x or better.

JUMPING TO GAME

The two-club bid indicates a hand that *might* play in game; it does not commit the partnership to game. Likewise, after a two-club response, opener's bid of two hearts or two spades does not indicate whether he has maximum or minimum point count. Therefore, either partner must be alert to get to game on his next bid if the hand belongs there. Responder bids game with 10 points or slightly less if there is a major-suit fit. Here are a few sample sequences:

1. Opener has a maximum or at least average notrump:

a.	NORTH	SOUTH		b.	NORTH	SOUTH
	1 NT	2 ♣			1 NT	2 ♣
	2 ♠	3 ♠			2 ♡	2 NT
	4 ♠				3 NT	

2. Responder has about 10 points:

a.	NORTH	SOUTH		b.	NORTH	SOUTH
	1 NT	2 ♣			1 NT	2 ♣
	2 ♠	4 ♠			2 ◇	3 NT

If responder had fewer points, he would bid three spades in Hand 2a and two notrump in Hand 2b.

Some more examples will illustrate the situations we have described. In the first three cases partner opens one notrump:

1. ♠ 10 5   ♡ Q 7 2   ◇ 8 3   ♣ A Q 10 4 3 2
Bid three notrump. The clubs should run, making nine tricks at notrump an easy affair. Two clubs (or three clubs) would be pointless. You have too much to settle for a club part-score.

2. ♠ K J 8 3 2   ♡ 5   ◇ K 10 3   ♣ J 10 6 5
Bid two clubs. Stayman will solve both your problems—where to play and how high. If partner happens to show four spades, you will jump to the spade game. If he bids two hearts (or two diamonds), you will reply with two spades, showing a 5-carder and a fairly good hand (else you would have bid two spades immediately). Now if partner raises spades, you will go on to four. If he bids two notrump, denying a good spade fit, you can let him play there (or go to three notrump *if* you have supreme confidence in his dummy technique).

3. ♠ A Q 8 6 2   ♡ Q 4 2   ◇ Q 4 2   ♣ 9 4
Bid three notrump. This is clearly the most sensible action. Your hand is not really unbalanced and you have honors in three suits, so why go out of your way to look for a 10-trick contract? Occasionally partner has a hand that will make four spades and not three notrump opposite yours, but against this is the

risk that Stayman may give your opponents a blueprint of their best defense. For example, if clubs are the weak spot in your combined holding, the next opponent might double your two-club Stayman response as a lead-director. Then, if you do not have a spade fit, you might be unable to make notrump, too.

4. ♠ 6 5   ♡ Q 10 5 4   ◇ K 5 4   ♣ A J 7 2
The bidding has been:

PARTNER	YOU
1 NT	2 ♣
2 ♠	?

Very technically your correct bid is three clubs (if played as forcing; otherwise, three diamonds). This forces another bid from partner, and you will eventually land in game—at either hearts or notrump. The three-club (or three-diamond) bid does not necessarily show the minor suit.

Now that you know the correct bid, forget it! It is the losingest bid you can make with an average partner. He might pass three clubs or three diamonds in a daze, or raise you to four. It is far safer just to bid three notrump and forget the 4-4 heart possibility (that's all it is).

5. ♠ 6 5   ♡ Q 10 5 4   ◇ J 5 4   ♣ A J 7 2
The bidding has been the same as in Hand 4.
Bid two notrump. This time you are not strong enough to insist on game. If partner has a maximum, he will get you to game by bidding three hearts over two notrump (if he has four hearts) or by bidding three notrump himself. And if he does not have a maximum, you have stayed out of trouble. Two notrump should be almost as good as three hearts, even if he has a heart fit. The important thing is to keep out of an unlikely game.

6. ♠ 5 2   ♡ Q J 10 7 4   ◇ A 5 2   ♣ J 5 3
The bidding has been:

PARTNER	YOU
1 NT	2 ♣
2 ♠	?

Bid two notrump. You'd like to bid three hearts and show the 5-carder, but this would commit you to game. If partner has a maximum, he will get you to game anyhow, and, of course, you will most cheerfully raise a three-heart bid.

7. ♠ 5 2   ♡ K J 10 8 2   ◇ A Q 4   ♣ 6 5 3
The bidding has been the same as in Hand 6.
Bid three hearts. This time you have the tickets to insist on game, and partner will almost certainly read this bid as forcing and know it promises five hearts. If the latter inference is beyond him, you will at least get to *some* game. If partner's bid is three notrump, it should suit you just as well.

To sum up, the Stayman Convention offers three principal advantages:

1. It smokes out a 4-4 (or sometimes a 5-3) major-suit fit which generally offers a better play for game.
2. It permits a suit sign-off at the two-level on an unbalanced weak responding hand.
3. As a temporizing bid, two clubs gives you time to determine whether an unbalanced borderline responding hand should go for part-score or game (or slam) and in what suit.

KNOW THY PARTNER

The Stayman Convention becomes a wicked boomerang if your partner is not familiar with it. There is plenty of opportunity to get your signals crossed. Therefore, don't attempt to teach it to your partner at the table.

Whenever you conclude your partner and Stayman do not mix, you and he should settle one pertinent point in advance—whether to play a response of two in a suit as a one-round forcing bid or a weakness sign-off.

Overcalls

Q. When is an opening bid not an opening bid?

A. When an opponent has already opened the bidding.

This riddle is the key to understanding the overcall. (Throughout this book I use the word "overcall" to mean a bid just high enough to top the last opposing bid, as in the sequences one spade-two diamonds, one club-one spade. If the bid skips a level of bidding, as in one club-*two* spades, it becomes a *jump* overcall.) There is a substantial advantage, and no great risk, in opening the bidding. But once an opponent beats you to the punch, you'd better readjust your thinking.

No self-respecting bridge player likes to keep silent on a hand with fair values. Yet many a hand is worth an opening bid but too risky for an overcall.

Contrast the two for a moment. As opening bidder, you announce some 14 points or more, begin a probe for the best trump suit, and set the stage for part-score, game, or slam. If an opponent doubles, it is for take-out; rarely is a profitable penalty inflicted on an opening bid.

How different the overcall. When the enemy starts the auction, you must recognize that slam is probably out of the question, game is unlikely, and you may not even be able to buy the hand for a part-score. On the other hand, you risk much more than the opener. Your left-hand opponent can double in a flash with just a fair trump holding and a few scattered honors, because his partner's opening bid has promised certain minimum defensive values. Thus a double usually writes *finis* for you; your bid has set the trump suit and the double says the opponents like it fine.

At best, a poor overcall gives the enemy a fielder's choice. They can rack it up by doubling, or use the information to proceed merrily on to their optimum contract—and then play the cards as if they had eyes.

Why overcall at all? Generally speaking, there are four objectives that can justify an overcall:

1. *To direct a lead against an eventual opposing contract.*
2. *To try to outbid the opponents with a fair-to-good hand.* It may turn out that your side has the balance of power. If not, your overcall may make the other team sell out too cheaply, or go one trick too high.
3. *To protect the chance for game.* Some hands produce game even after an adverse opening bid, provided partner can offer encouragement. But you won't find out unless you get into the bidding early.
4. *To keep the enemy guessing.* Occasionally a dubious overcall is good tactics. Like a bluff in poker, it earns the distrust of the opponents.

There is a limit to the risk you should take. The following hand is instructive:

$$\spadesuit \text{ J 5 3} \qquad \heartsuit \text{ Q 4} \qquad \diamondsuit \text{ A Q 7 5 4} \qquad \clubsuit \text{ A 6 2}$$

Neither side is vulnerable and your right-hand opponent opens one spade.

Do you overcall two diamonds? You have the values for an opening bid and might justify an overcall with any of the first three reasons above.

The gentleman who held these cards in a rubber game chose to overcall, was promptly doubled, and went for 700 points. Later he discovered the opponents had no game of their own.

Honor tricks, Quick Tricks, high-card points—none of these has anything to do with overcalls. An overcall does not promise *defensive* strength; it must have *playing* strength—either a respectable suit or a two-suiter.

The safety factor is influenced by the bidding level and vulnerability. Opponents are often reluctant to leave in a double at the one level, fearing it will produce too small a set to be worthwhile. No such compunction exists about a two-level overcall, particularly in a minor suit, which will not cost game if the contract is made.

A 4-card suit offers small safety, and is seldom used for even a one-level overcall. At the two level, you usually want *more* than a 5-card suit.

Vulnerability is a gauge for measuring potential loss against potential gain. Your loss, if you are doubled and find a blank dummy, should not exceed the value of an opposing game. Thus, not vulnerable, you need within three probable tricks of your contract; vulnerable, within two. Put another way, you fix your maximum loss at 500 points.

In figuring winners, expect neither a good fit with partner nor a horrible trump break against you. Assume average distribution (or slightly worse, in the interest of safety), and then tot up the tricks that are reasonably yours.

Suppose we start with the weakest possible overcall and work our way up:

1. ♠ A Q J 8 5   ♡ 9 4 2   ◇ 7 6   ♣ 10 5 4
Not vulnerable.
Bid one spade over one club, one diamond or one heart. This is a good overcall.
It may inhibit the opponents; if they credit you with more than you have, it
may keep them out of a makable game. More important, you signal your partner
to lead spades against an opposing notrump contract (and probably against a
suit contract, as well).

2. ♠ A 10 7 5 4   ♡ K 3   ◇ K Q 4   ♣ 7 6 3
Vulnerable or not vulnerable. Right-hand opponent bids one club.
Overcall one spade. The suit is no great shakes and you don't particularly want
it led, but the hand is too good for you to stay out; partner may easily have
enough for game. If you pass and your left-hand opponent bids, your partner
will have a tough time entering the auction at the two-level even if he has a
fairly good hand, and you certainly cannot back in later after first passing.

3. ♠ 5   ♡ K 5   ◇ 9 7 6 3   ♣ A Q J 9 7 6
Not vulnerable. Right-hand opponent bids one spade.
Bid two clubs. Two-level overcalls should be at least 1 winner better than the
one-level variety. Here you want a club led in defense and you have some
remote hope for game if partner can now volunteer strong action.

4. ♠ 7 5   ♡ 8 6   ◇ A K Q   ♣ J 8 7 6 4 3
Not vulnerable. Right-hand opponent bids one spade.
Pass. You shouldn't get too severely hurt if doubled at two clubs, but there is
no point to the overcall. You certainly don't want clubs led, and game is remote
unless partner can act independently.

5. ♠ Q J 5   ♡ A Q 8 7 2   ◇ A 6 3   ♣ 8 5
Vulnerable. Right-hand opponent bids one spade.
Pass. Thirteen points, but not enough playing strength. *A two-level vulnerable
overcall is never made without a pretty substantial hand.*

6. ♠ 5   ♡ K Q 10 9 7 5   ◇ K J 10   ♣ J 4 2
Vulnerable. Right-hand opponent bids one spade.
Bid two hearts. Contrast with Hand 5. Here you have fewer high-card points,
but you can figure on 6 probable winners.

THE ONE-NOTRUMP OVERCALL

Don't tamper with this bid. Show it the same respect as an *opening* one-
notrump bid. In fact, the one-notrump overcall should show the same 15-
to-18-point range. However, since a hand of this strength also qualifies for
a take-out double, the one-notrump overcall implies that 1) the bid suit is

doubly stopped, and 2) the support for the unbid major suit or suits is indifferent at best. Two examples:

1. ♠ A Q 10   ♡ K 5   ♢ Q J 4 3   ♣ A 10 9 3
Right-hand opponent bids one spade.
Bid one notrump.

2. ♠ Q 3   ♡ A 10 5   ♢ K J 5   ♣ A Q 9 6 3
Right-hand opponent bids one diamond.
Bid one notrump.

RESPONSES TO A SUIT OVERCALL

Since your partner promises no particular high-card strength for his overcall, you shouldn't venture into the fray without reason. Your first task is to gauge his strength. The safest course is to figure him for only the minimum playing strength for the actual vulnerability and bidding level. But keep your ears open; if the vulnerable opponents are bidding strongly, partner has probably stretched to find an overcall, nonvulnerable.

If you have sufficient values to confuse or compete with the opponents, jump right into the bidding, preferably by raising partner's suit. Remember, his overcall denies any real interest in *your* suit, whatever it is, and a trump fit will be most welcome news to him. Normal trump support for an overcall is three small cards, but even J-x suffices for a two-level overcall. For preemptive reasons, the modern tendency is to raise an overcall very lightly when *good* trump support is held.

An overcall is not meant to be rescued. You should at least wait until it is doubled before considering heroics. After all, you are halfway out of the woods when your right-hand opponent passes, and you may very well get by the other opponent. But as soon as you come in with some new suit, you permit the opponents two potshots at you.

There is a place for the suit take-out after an overcall. It should show a good suit, no good fit with partner, and a hand of some values. In brief, it is a forward-going bid, suggesting an alternate contract and game hopes, but by no means forcing. Even a jump response to an overcall is not absolutely forcing; besides, it is an awkward call that crowds the bidding.

The only forcing bid after an overcall is a cue-bid in the opponent's suit. This is a convenience call, for it lets both partners relax and bid naturally thereafter. The cue-bid indicates general strength plus a desire to explore, but it is not an absolute guarantee of any control in the adverse suit. For example, in the sequence one spade—two clubs—pass—two spades, the last bid could be made on three small spades (but the rest of the hand should make up for this). Let's try out these theories on a few hands. You are South:

1. ♠ 7 3 2   ♡ A Q 10 5 4   ◇ K 6 3   ♣ 7 4

WEST	NORTH	EAST	SOUTH
1♣	1♠	Pass	?

Bid two spades. You have ample trump support and enough meat to make some move. There is no purpose in mentioning the hearts for the spade suit is certainly satisfactory.

2. ♠ 8 5 3   ♡ 4 2   ◇ K 9 6 3   ♣ Q 10 4 2

WEST	NORTH	EAST	SOUTH
1♠	2◇	Pass	?

Bid three diamonds. Here is an example of the light raise with good trump support. You don't expect to go places, but it is good strategy to make it difficult for the opponents to reach their probable major-suit game.

3. ♠ 10 5 4   ♡ 3   ◇ Q J 8 6 4 2   ♣ K 6 3

WEST	NORTH	EAST	SOUTH
1♠	2♡	Pass	?

Pass—and quickly, too. Don't rescue an undoubled overcall. If the ax falls, you should still pass with this hand opposite a reliable partner. With a very flighty partner, you might chance a three-diamond rescue on the theory that mayhem would be committed on his two-heart bid and the hope that, with you at the helm, three diamonds will fare much better.

4. ♠ 10 5   ♡ 3   ◇ A K Q J 6 2   ♣ 10 9 5 4

WEST	NORTH	EAST	SOUTH
1♠	2♡	Pass	?

Bid three diamonds—not as a rescue, but in hopes. This could be all partner needs to bid three notrump, and you can contribute 6 fine tricks to that contract.

5. ♠ A 5 4   ♡ A K J 9 7 3   ◇ Q 5   ♣ Q 6

WEST	NORTH	EAST	SOUTH
1♠	2♣	Pass	?

Bid two spades. This cue-bid insures reaching game (unless partner's overcall was the super-hungry type) and provides for all bidding eventualities. Partner's next bid will clarify his hand, and you can then show your hearts comfortably. Your other choice is to jump immediately to three hearts; however, this is not completely forcing and might take you past a makable three-notrump contract by wasting the extra bidding level.

Since a notrump overcall denotes the same strength as a notrump opening, the responses are the same, including the Stayman Convention.

JUMP OVERCALLS

In the very early days of contract, the single-jump overcall was used as a strong bid and a game invitation, requesting partner to assist with as little as one playing trick or one high-card trick. However, as early as the middle thirties most good players began to come around to the opinion that using the jump overcall as a strong bid was unnecessary. Today only a few diehards among major players so employ it. Although I play several rubbers daily, only two or three times a year do I encounter a hand on which I feel the need for a strong jump overcall. And on those few hands, either a take-out double or a cue-bid in the opponents' suit—or even a simple overcall, if vulnerable—proves an adequate substitute. But the occasion to use the jump overcall as a semi-pre-emptive, non-strength-showing bid comes up very frequently.

A further discussion of my case for the weak jump overcall is reserved for a subsequent chapter. The important thing to note here is that which jump overcall—strong or weak—you use is not of sufficient importance to jeopardize partnership rapport. If your partner likes the strong jump overcall, tell him you will cooperate any time he makes one. As for you, two courses are open: 1) You can simply tell him you will make your jump overcalls strong also since the occasion probably won't come up anyway, or 2) If partner is an agreeable sort, tell him you use the weak jump overcall so he should not take yours too seriously and should raise only on distinct values. I have gotten on very well with many partners on this compromise basis. Naturally, if you are permitted to use the weak jump overcall only under sufferance, you are particularly careful with it.

The Take-out Double

The take-out double is the granddaddy of all artificial bids. It has been around so long that it has become an integral part of the game; even the inexperienced player knows its meaning.

This action, as much as any other, epitomizes winning partnership bridge, in that it initiates an auction that demands the full cooperation of both partners.

Other authors have laid down abundant ground rules—what is the minimum strength needed, what shape the hand should be, how to distinguish a take-out double from a penalty double. I want to emphasize the importance of judgment in applying these rules.

The take-out double offers two elements of safety. It enables you to get into the bidding early without undue risk, and at the same time to test game possibilities without losing your shirt. It fits in admirably with the winning tactics of being reasonably aggressive on the first round.

Note the distinction between an overcall and a take-out double: an overcall sets the trump suit; a take-out double seeks advice. It follows that the overcall is based primarily on playing strength, the take-out double on a combination of high-card strength and distribution.

If an opening one-spade bid is made on your right, and you hold

♠ 5   ♡ A 7 4 3   ◇ K Q 5 4   ♣ A J 8 3

everyone knows a take-out double is automatic. It would be foolhardy to guess which 4-card suit to play when you can safely ask partner's help in picking the spot.

Now let's examine two less obvious types of take-out double.

First, there is the take-out double to achieve relative safety in case partner has a really bad hand:

♠ 7 3   ♡ A Q 6 4 2   ◇ K J 3   ♣ K 8 4

One spade is opened on your right; you are not vulnerable. If you are reasonably aggressive, you want to get into the bidding on this hand. (The same would hold true if you were vulnerable and the opponents had a part-score.) But with so little body to the hand, you have to protect yourself against catastrophe in the event that partner has nothing. Say you bid two hearts and are doubled on your left. You have had it! You have no place to go, and—more to the point—your partner, correctly, won't rescue you with some mediocre 5-card minor suit. For all he knows, you have a good playable heart suit, and a runout to three clubs or three diamonds could take a horrible beating.

But suppose you make a take-out double instead of the overcall. Now you have sharply cut your chances of being caught. If partner has the bad hand you are allowing for, he can respond in his better minor at the two-level, and you can gracefully retire. Likely as not, the opponents will be unable to double you there, and you have avoided the big set. You may not be able to buy the hand, but with relative safety you have made sure you haven't been talked out of anything. Can you ask more from one bid?

Second, there is the take-out double to show an independent suit in a good hand:

♠ A K J 9 6 2   ♡ A 8 4   ◇ K J   ♣ 7 2

One club is opened on your right; you are not vulnerable. A one-spade overcall is unthinkable with so much power. *Double first and bid your spades later.* Partner will then know you have good spades *and* considerable high-card strength—in other words, hopes for game. Even if you were vulnerable, the take-out double would be superior to the overcall. A vulnerable overcall indicates a good hand, but not necessarily so robust as this one.

The vulnerability situation dictates greater caution or more derring-do. To a lesser extent, knowledge of your partner's aggressiveness—or lack of it —should affect your decision.

SUIT RESPONSES

Although the meaning of the take-out double is widely understood, there is much confusion in the ranks about the meaning of the responses to it.

The prime culprit is the single jump in a new suit. Many players—even some fairly experienced ones—misconstrue this as a forcing bid. But this conception destroys the effectiveness of the take-out double.

Partner doubles an opening one-club bid, and you have this mess:

1. ♠ 9 6 4 2   ♡ 6 3 2   ◇ 5 3 2   ♣ 4 3 2

You have to respond one spade, like it or not. How, then, can you show this intermediate hand

2. ♠ K J 8 5 3   ♡ 10 4   ◇ K 10 9 8   ♣ J 5

except by a jump to two spades? If you play the jump to two spades as absolutely forcing, you arrive at game willy-nilly, even if partner started out with a minimum take-out double. If you strait-jacket your partnership in this fashion, you have to respond one spade on Hand 2—the same bid as on Hand 1. Since you may just as easily have Hand 1 as the superior Hand 2, how can partner know whether to make a further bid?

The case for an invitational—but not forcing—jump response is convincing. Then, after hearing a jump, partner can still pass with a minimum double, but is free to raise to three or four with a strong double. There are thousands of hands whose strength falls somewhere between that of Hands 1 and 2 above, and each has to be decided on its own merits.

Beware of pushing too hard to find a jump just because the bid is not a force:

♠ K 8 5 3 2   ♡ 8 7 4   ◇ Q J 3   ♣ 9 2

After partner doubles the opening one-club bid, you should be content with a one-spade response, even though you have certain values. You do not have to worry too much about missing a game if partner passes out one spade. Of course, if partner raises, you will find another bid.

Don't settle for a jump response after the double when you know you want to be in game—even opposite a minimum double.

♠ J 5   ♡ K J 10 8 7 3   ◇ A 4 2   ♣ 7 3

After partner doubles the opening one-club bid, bid four hearts directly.

61

There must be a good play for this contract, and partner might not be able to move over a mere two-heart invitation.

And with this hand

♠ K Q 7 5 4   ♡ A 10 3 2   ◇ Q 5   ♣ 6 3

cue-bid two clubs, the enemy's suit, after partner's double. This is, of course, a one-round force and indicates doubt as to where the hand should play. Partner is expected to name his best suit, and you will raise either major suit directly to game. If he bids two diamonds, you should be content to bid two spades, since you have already shown considerable strength. The two-spade bid still leaves room to explore for a heart or notrump game, as well as one in spades.

THE PENALTY PASS

You can pass your partner's take-out double and thereby convert it into a penalty double—but be sure you have a darn good chance to beat the contract. You need at least a fairly strong 6-card trump holding, such as Q-J-9-7-6-4, or a better 5-card holding, such as K-Q-10-9-7. Even then, if you have another favorable feature, such as a good 5-card major suit, think twice before giving up your chance for game.

Never pass out of fright. If you have a Yarborough, like Hand 1 on page 61, you are far better off at some low contract of your own than in letting the opponents make theirs—doubled and with overtricks. Moreover, passing a take-out double with such a hand destroys partnership confidence and can cost you additional points on later hands.

THE ONE-NOTRUMP RESPONSE

With a hopeless hand you naturally look for the cheapest response—and *that may easily turn out to be one notrump.* Many players attribute strength to a one-notrump response to a take-out double, regardless of the suit that was opened. But what other action makes sense with the following hand after partner doubles one spade?

1. ♠ Q 10 5 3   ♡ 7 4 3   ◇ 6 4 3   · ♣ 8 4 2

Bid one notrump. Lord knows, you have no strength—but partner shouldn't expect any, because *this is the cheapest bid available.*

Try the same hand with the black suits switched; and partner has doubled an opening one-club bid:

2. ♠ 8 4 2   ♡ 7 4 3   ◊ 6 4 3   ♣ Q 10 5 3

Bid one diamond. You don't have a suit, so you choose the cheapest 3-carder. If you bid one notrump over one club, doubled, partner has the right to look for some values, because you have passed over three other possible havens. In this case, you should hold something like:

♠ K 5 4   ♡ 10 4 3   ◊ K 9 7   ♣ Q 10 8 3

In short, the notrump response shows strength *only* when it skips over lower bids. However, be prepared to be hanged by partners who woodenly expect every notrump response to advertise strength. You'll get your revenge when you're their opponent.

AFTER A REDOUBLE

None of our leading lights has yet come out with a really clear analysis of the meaning of a "free" bid after an intervening redouble of partner's take-out double. Culbertson and others many years ago insisted that a pass here showed strength and a willingness to let the opponents play at the one-level redoubled. Other pundits intoned that a *bid* indicated a good hand.

I will meet this issue head-on: *both these treatments are artificial and unworkable.* Generally speaking, a player should pass when he has nothing to say and bid when he has a decent suit. His decision should be dictated by logic and the search for safety:

1. ♠ 10 8 6 4 3   ♡ 8 7 4 2   ◊ 6 5   ♣ 8 3

One heart – double – redouble – ?
Bid one spade. If you pass, partner may have three good spades and still be forced to take out one heart redoubled into two of a shaky minor. You are less likely to get doubled at one spade, and once two clubs or two diamonds gets the ax, the opponents will double any further bid. If you skip over the spade suit at the one-level by passing, you have shut the door in your own face. Partner should not infer any strength from your spade bid, since it is the *lowest possible bid* over one heart.

2. ♠ 10 8 7 5 3   ♡ J 4 2   ◇ 8 7 3   ♣ 9 2

One club — double — redouble — ?
Pass. Partner may have a fine diamond or heart suit which you can stand, and it would be criminal to shut him out at the one-level. You should be delighted that the redouble frees you of the obligation to respond, so you can keep out of partner's way. A spade bid on this sequence would show something considerably better than 10-x-x-x-x in the suit and a bust.

3. ♠ K 10 8 7 3   ♡ 8 4   ◇ K 4 2   ♣ 7 6 2

One club — double — redouble — ?
Bid one spade, ignoring the redouble. You have a decent spade suit and some strength to show, so don't be bashful. Partner will know you have something, since your bid skips over one diamond and one heart.

4. ♠ K 8 6 3   ♡ Q J 4   ◇ K 8 4   ♣ Q 10 3

One club — double — redouble — ?
Pass, and play the waiting game. This comes under the heading of strategy. You're sure this hand belongs to you and your partner, but you're not sure how. You want to see how partner takes out one club redoubled, and then you can raise him (or do what you will) after he picks the suit. If the opponents get even a wee bit frisky, you have a surprise waiting for them.

The tactics recommended throughout this chapter are best with any partner, even a total stranger.

After an Opposing Take-out Double

In Chapter 9, I dealt with the times your side makes a take-out double. Now we turn to the take-out double the enemy makes after your partner opens the bidding. This may seem a very small phase of contract-bridge bidding, but it is burdened with so many clichés and contradictions that it deserves a chapter all its own.

You know the situation: partner opens with one of a suit, your right-hand opponent doubles, and you bid something. In any but the most expert game this sequence is sure to draw forth an articulate post-mortem. Usually the opening bidder, for all the world acting as if he were quoting from the Koran, scolds, "But, partner, I *had* to play you for nothing; you *bid* over the take-out double."

Well, then, if a bid shows "nothing," a pass must surely show "something!" The bidding structure has been turned upside down—and the opponents score all the points.

There is a tiny germ of truth here, but it has been distorted beyond recognition by some of our ambitious but inexperienced bridge aficionados. Whenever you bid over an opposing double you *limit* the strength of your hand by denying the strength to redouble. However, that is a far cry from "nothing". Oh yes, there are times when you rescue—with a long suit of your own and a singleton or void in partner's suit—out of fear of a business pass by doubler's partner. Please note that this is the exception, not the rule. It does *not* mean that a player who passes over a double is surely showing a better hand than one who bids. When you think a moment about it, you can see the idiocy of this notion.

This area of bidding will seem less complicated if you bear in mind the basic over-all objective of partnership bidding: to show as much of the hand as is possible and seems pertinent. Frequently this requires more than one bid, so you must try to anticipate opportunities that can be grasped without danger on future bidding rounds.

Expert bridge theory stipulates that every bid should have its own meaning and use. It is equally true that the wider the choice of available bids the more accurate the message of any one. Thus after a take-out double— since this is a free country—opening bidder's partner can pass, redouble, bid one of a suit or one notrump, or jump in a suit or notrump. The choice of action should depend on the exact hand he holds, but in the average bridge game this principle is abundantly honored in the breach.

With a very good hand you must redouble immediately, regardless of what action you intend to take later. In general, you should not pass with a strong hand, planning to back in later. This tactic is rapidly dying out among successful players. If the hand qualifies, the expert redoubles; if the hand is not quite that strong, he tends to find an immediate bid.

You lose nothing by redoubling with a strong hand. If the opponents are in trouble, your redouble keeps them on the hook. And it tells your partner your story: unless he has opened a psychic, the hand clearly belongs to your side.

What strength do you need for a redouble? Thirteen points in high cards, regardless of distribution or fit with partner's suit, constitutes a "compulsory" redouble. (Freak, very lopsided hands are exceptions to all rules and call for special treatment.) When you have good support for partner's suit, 7 or 8 points may suffice.

Here are a few examples of sound redoubles without support for partner's suit. In each case partner opens with one spade and your right-hand opponent doubles:

1. ♠ J 5   ♡ A Q 8 7 6   ◇ K 5 4   ♣ Q 4 3

2. ♠ 5 4   ♡ K 8 5   ◇ A K Q 6 3   ♣ 7 6 5

3. ♠ 8   ♡ A K 6   ◇ A 10 4 3   ♣ Q 10 7 4 3

4. ♠ J 2   ♡ A Q J 10 4 3   ◇ A 6 5   ♣ Q 8

When you have three cards to an honor in support of partner's suit, you may redouble with as little as 10 high-card points. Again, partner opens with one spade and your right-hand opponent doubles:

5. ♠ J 8 7   ♡ A 5 4   ◇ K J 5 3   ♣ Q 6 2

6. ♠ K 3 2   ♡ A 8   ◇ Q J 7 2   ♣ 8 6 4 2

7. ♠ Q 6 4   ♡ A 6 4 2   ◇ 4 2   ♣ K J 5 2

The following hands have good trump support, and the point-count requirement is correspondingly reduced. As above, partner opens with one spade and your right-hand opponent doubles:

8. ♠ K 10 7 5   ♡ Q 10 5 3   ◇ K 10 8 7   ♣ 6

9. ♠ A 10 7 6 5   ♡ K 4 3   ◇ 8 7   ♣ 8 7 6

10. ♠ K 10 6 5 4   ♡ 8   ◇ K J 10 8   ♣ 5 3 2

11. ♠ A 8 7 6   ♡ 6   ◇ K Q J 4 3 2   ♣ A 5

Instead of the redouble, you might choose a raise to three or four spades on Hands 8, 9, and 10 for strategic reasons—the vulnerability situation or special knowledge of your opponents, for example.

Your action after the redouble helps your partner visualize your hand. With a powerhouse like Hand 11, you'll obviously want to keep bidding strongly and test for slam. With a minimum redouble, as in Hand 8, you should make no further strong move.

Having redoubled, you *cannot* pass out the opponent's subsequent suit take-out if you are the last hand to speak. There is no point in redoubling if you allow the opponents to buy the hand undoubled at such a cheap level.

Your redouble guarantees you will take some action in such a situation. In fact, your partner usually passes the opponent's suit take-out around to you if he has no clear-cut action of his own. However, he is not *forced* to pass after the opponent's suit bid, although many players mistakenly believe so. He may be able to double the suit take-out on his own initiative. Or he may further describe his hand if it is completely unsuited for defensive play; there is no point in giving you a chance to double for penalties if he cannot let your double stand. For example:

1. ♠ A Q J 9 6 3   ♡ 7 4   ◇ K Q J 2   ♣ 3

Your partner is dealer. One spade — double — redouble — two clubs
          ?

He should bid two spades. He has no intention of letting a doubled two-club contract stand, and this is a cheap opportunity to indicate his excellent spade suit.

However, opener should beware of bidding at this juncture just because his suit is rebiddable:

2. ♠ A Q 10 6 4   ♡ Q J 5   ◇ K Q 4   ♣ 8 5

Your partner is dealer. One spade — double — redouble — two clubs
?

He should pass; if you double two clubs, his club doubleton is sufficient to let it play there. Should he impulsively bid two spades instead, he may find you with Hand 3 shown earlier in the chapter. Two clubs doubled would take a real ride, but game is not such a good bet on these two combined hands.

WHEN TO IGNORE THE TAKE-OUT DOUBLE

This phase of bidding seems to throw the average player. Many times the most logical course is to ignore the double and make your natural bid. This is true whenever you have a hand too weak for a redouble but *too good for you to risk having to stay completely out of the bidding.*

♠ A Q 9 7 5   ♡ 9 6 3   ◇ Q 10 5   ♣ 7 3

You are vulnerable; opponents are non-vulnerable. Partner opens one heart, and the next player doubles. Certainly you lack the requirements for a re-double. But do you want to pass and hear a two-club bid on your left, a pass from partner, and a three-club raise on your right? You are smack in the middle of a guessing game. It is highly dangerous to bid either three hearts or three spades at this point, and yet you hate to sell out without ever opening your mouth and possibly let the opponents get away with some pre-emptive bluffing. The simple, natural solution is to bid one spade on the first round to show you have a little something but not enough to redouble. This bid does not preclude 3-card heart support. Once you have said your say, partner is in a better position to bid or to double if the opposition gets persistent.

The one firm rule in bidding over a redouble is that there is no firm rule. For example, take the last example but with only the opponents vulnerable. Now a pass might work out well. The opponents may be en route to trouble (the doubler's partner may even respond in spades). In any event you can put more credence in their vulnerable bidding and will be better able to decide whether to step in later. Note that the pass violates our previous warning against passing first and coming in later. But we suggest it as a possibility on this vulnerability.

THE ONE-NOTRUMP RESPONSE

The one-notrump response after an opposing take-out double has grad-ually evolved into a beautifully precise bid with good players—all without any formal round-table discussions or symposiums.

When vulnerable, it requires a balanced hand pattern of 4-3-3-3 or 4-4-3-2 (almost always lacking four cards in partner's suit), and 8 or 9 points. A hand with 10 "bad" points (a holding of A-A-Q or A-K-K is a "good" 10-pointer) also qualifies—something like:

♠ K J 4   ♡ Q 5 2   ◇ Q 8 4   ♣ Q 4 3 2

Since the double removes the need to keep the bidding open, there is no purpose to a one-notrump reply on a hand of from 5 to 7 points; you can pass instead. At the other end of the scale, you do not have to bid one notrump with as much as 11 or 12 points, as you occasionally must do when there is a pass on your right. The double has changed all that, and you now can redouble to show this kind of hand. Since there are more appropriate actions for 5-to-7-point hands and 11- or 12-pointers, the one-notrump response over a double is reserved for the in-between range. Thus your partner knows exactly where he stands, and you are spared the agonizing second thoughts that plague the player who passes in this situation.

When not vulnerable, more latitude is permitted. This is particularly true if the opponents are vulnerable, for you may sense a juicy penalty in the offing and want to play possum to guide the opponents into the trap. But when vulnerable, get yourself off the hook by making that one-notrump bid right then and there.

In each of the following examples both sides are vulnerable; partner bids one heart and your right-hand opponent doubles.

1. ♠ Q 7 6   ♡ Q 9 6 5 4   ◇ 8 4 2   ♣ 6 4
Bid two hearts. The trump length justifies this mild attempt to shut out the opponents.

2. ♠ Q 5 4   ♡ Q 8 7 6   ◇ 6 4 2   ♣ 6 5 3
Pass. Too dangerous for even a pre-emptive raise. Remember, you are vulnerable, as well as the opponents.

3. ♠ K 3 2   ♡ 8 6 4   ◇ 7 6 5 4 3   ♣ 8 2
Pass. What else?

4. ♠ A 3 2   ♡ 3 2   ◇ J 8 3 2   ♣ J 6 5 4
Pass. You should be willing to be shut out unless partner offers further encouragement.

5. ♠ 8   ♡ K Q 8 7 6   ◇ Q 4 3 2   ♣ 6 4 2
Bid three hearts. Your failure to redouble warns partner to go to game only if he has distinct additional values.

6. ♠ K Q 10 8 7   ♡ 8 2   ◇ Q 7 6   ♣ J 3 2

Bid one spade. A typical convenience bid, ignoring the double. Since partner may be short in spades and you are short in hearts, it would be dangerous to pass and come in later. And you have too much to sell out without opening your mouth.

7. ♠ 6 5 4   ♡ 5 4   ◇ K Q 10 8 7 5   ♣ Q 4

Bid two diamonds. Another natural convenience bid. The strength of the diamond suit warrants it.

8. ♠ Q 3 2   ♡ J 8   ◇ K Q 10 8 4 3   ♣ A 8

Redouble. With the additional ace and jack, you are too strong for a two-diamond bid, which would deny the values for a redouble. Under certain circumstances, a pass might be good strategy, but the redouble gets the nod when you are playing with just any partner.

9. ♠ K 8 7   ♡ J 8 7   ◇ A 6 5 4   ♣ J 3 2

Bid one notrump. A typical hand for this vulnerable bid. You are off the spot, and the rest is up to partner.

10. ♠ Q 6 4   ♡ J 4 3   ◇ A 8 7 6   ♣ A 8 7

Redouble. Eleven points is too much for the notrump call, and this is surely not the hand for passing and coming in later.

11. ♠ 8 7   ♡ 10 8 4   ◇ A Q 10 8 5 3   ♣ 7 3

Bid two diamonds. Come in now, because it could get sticky later. If partner rebids his hearts, you may even see fit to support him.

12. ♠ 7 5   ♡ 6 5 4   ◇ A Q 10 7 6   ♣ J 4 3

Pass. The diamonds are not so good that they should be shown at the two-level. If the pass keeps you out of the auction, you need have no misgivings.

13. ♠ K 10 9 8 7   ♡ 2   ◇ 5 4 3 2   ♣ 8 5 2

Bid one spade, more or less as a rescue.

14. ♠ 3 2   ♡ 2   ◇ A K J 10 5 3 2   ♣ Q J 7

Bid three diamonds. A jump shift in this situation is considered a one-round force by some, barely an urge by others and a pure weakness pre-empt by still others. (I subscribe to the middle school.) If partner wears my school tie, he will pass with a minimum hand and no fit in your suit, but will carry on with additional values, knowing you have a strong suit. No matter which way he interprets the bid, no serious harm can result. The one thing clear is that failure to redouble limits your hand.

15. ♠ 7 ♡ K J 10 7 6 5 4 ◇ 8 3 2 ♣ 6 5

Redouble or pass. Four hearts is the book bid, but it just cannot work; with your singleton spade and extreme heart length, you can't shut the opponents out. Therefore, I recommend a fancy redouble or, as second choice, a pass. Paradoxical as it may seem, this increases your chances of buying the hand at a lower level; also, you will have a better idea of how far to go after hearing more rounds of bidding.

16. ♠ Q J 8 ♡ J 3 ◇ K 10 8 3 ♣ J 10 8 6

Bid one notrump. Another example of the convenience call.

17. ♠ K 10 7 ♡ Q 6 ◇ K 8 3 ♣ 10 8 6 4 2

Bid one notrump. Still another example of this precision tool, this time with a 5-card minor suit thrown in.

I could go on with many more examples to point up the almost infinite variations resulting from vulnerability, part-scores, and the bidding level at which you must enter. However, the important thing is to get rid of the clichés and hokum that surround this subject and to substitute common sense and anticipation of how the bidding may develop.

The approach I have outlined is the safest and most effective with any partner, even a total stranger. Since bidding after an opposing take-out double is not commonly brought up in pre-game discussions, it is all the more important for your actions to be firmly grounded in clear-headed logic.

Slam Bidding

There are few greater thrills in bridge than bidding a difficult slam and then bringing it home in triumph. Generous bonuses reward this achievement and such bonuses, in some games—we are told—are redeemable in cold cash.

The average player covets the slam but knows blissfully little of its nature.

Items:

Frequency of slams—A reasonable play for slam occurs about once in ten deals—for your side, once in twenty deals.

Limitation of your system—The slam bonus is not great enough to offset the fact that you have a reasonable play for game six times as often as you do for slam. Thus, a winning system must be geared *primarily* to bidding the reasonable games and staying out of the unreasonable ones. For this reason, the standard American system assigns a lower priority to slam bidding. This does not mean slam bidding is cumbersome or slipshod; just don't expect perfection, that's all. Be content to master the various common-sense slam-bidding tools and to use them judiciously.

When to bid a slam—Only when you have at least a fifty-fifty chance of making a slam should you bid it, because if you go down one you lose just about what you hoped to gain. For example, if you bid a slam in spades and go down one, vulnerable, you lose 100 points; if you bid game in spades and make an overtrick, you score 650 points. The difference is 750 points, exactly equal to the vulnerable small-slam bonus.

It's not strictly true, as some writers have postulated, that "Slam is just game with a couple of overtricks." It does you no good to have twelve sure tricks on tap if the opponents take the first two.

For a reasonable slam play, you need first-round control in three suits and second-round control in the fourth. If you lack these requirements, be satisfied with game. A favorable lead may net you two overtricks, but would the opponents have been so conciliatory if you had *bid* the slam? Remember, a slam bid changes their objective as well as yours.

Even with the required controls, you are not out of the woods. It is fine to win the first trick of a suit, but you also need a parking place for the other cards in the suit. In short, you need either a runnable suit that provides discards or such a wealth of high cards in the combined hands that you have twelve tricks on sheer power.

Most slams evolve gradually. First game is apparent. Next the partners explore for controls, and finally one bids the slam if he thinks there are 12 winners as well as sufficient controls. The trick is to test for slam without jeopardizing a sure game. That brings us to the strong opening two-bid.

THE STRONG TWO-BID

This tool, as much as any other, sets the stage for slam. Also, it provides the oft-overlooked advantage of keeping you out of an *unmakable* slam. But this advantage is just theoretical if you fail to open your two-bid.

♠ 5   ♡ K Q   ◇ A 10   ♣ A K Q 7 6 5 3 2

In a recent rubber game my partner chose to open this tidy little number with a humble one-club. I was able to keep the bidding open (just barely) with one spade. That was sufficient, however, to catapult him into Blackwood, which located my one ace. He thereby found a slam contract for which there was virtually no play.

Later I suggested that an opening bid of *two* clubs would have avoided this catastrophe. It would have granted me full partnership rights and he would not have had to atone for an early underbid by a later solo flight to the stratosphere.

"With my distribution, somebody at the table was sure to be able to bid over one club," he countered. What sort of negative thinking is that? If you have the makings of a two-bid, for heaven's sake say the magic words.

Experience and common sense tell you when you have a legitimate two-bid. You don't need an absolutely certain game in your own hand. If all you need from partner is a bare smattering of high cards, or a decent fit in your suit (or one of your suits), you have good reason to open with two. However, your two-bid should guarantee at least four of the eight aces and kings barring some real freak; otherwise there may be an overlap in high cards that may trap partner into bidding an unmakable slam.

On each of the following hands, the optimum contract can best be reached by means of an opening two-bid in the longest suit. (With two good suits of equal length, as in Hands 3 and 8, open with the higher-ranking one.):

1. ♠ K Q J 10 8 6   ♡ A   ◇ K Q 10 9   ♣ K 3

2. ♠ 7 5   ♡ A K J 5   ◇ A K Q J 10 6   ♣ 5

3. ♠ A Q 10 7 3   ♡ A 4   ◇ A K Q 7 3   ♣ 4

4. ♠ None   ♡ A Q J 10 8 7 5 3   ◇ A 5   ♣ K J 10

5. ♠ Q 4   ♡ A K   ◇ K J 10 3   ♣ A K Q 10 3

6. ♠ A 10 8 7 6 3   ♡ A K   ◇ A Q J 9 8   ♣ None

7. ♠ A   ♡ A K 10 9 6 4   ◇ K J 9 3   ♣ A J

8. ♠ A K J 10 7   ♡ A Q J 10 9   ◇ 7   ♣ K 5

9. ♠ A 5   ♡ A K 9 8 7 4 3 2   ◇ 4   ♣ K 8

RESPONSES TO THE TWO-BID

There are two types of response to a two-bid. One, known as "Aces Over Two-Bids," stipulates that if responder has an ace, he must reply in that suit, regardless of its length; if he has no ace, he must respond with two notrump. This reduces responder to an automaton, but works beautifully whenever the opener has a self-sufficient suit and a void and needs only to know which ace, if any, partner holds. However, such hands crop up seldom. Still, this method is playable, if you go for that kind of thing.

The second is endorsed by most recognized top-flight players, and I go along with it enthusiastically. This is the natural-response method: on any hand with values, the responder makes his natural bid regardless of aces. Two notrump is a negative bid—showing less than 7 points (or as much as 9 points without ace or king). This method lets responder describe the most pertinent feature of his hand, and any time a player can exercise his judgment the partnership functions that much more smoothly.

Interestingly, the natural response may well show an ace in the suit bid. I'd guess that chances are better than two to one that you hold the ace in the suit you bid. You wouldn't bid the suit unless you had some high honor.

Sometimes you go out of your way to show an ace:

1. ♠ A 5 4 3   ♡ J 9 3   ◊ Q J 5 2   ♣ 8 7
Partner opens with two hearts.
Bid two spades. When you later raise hearts, partner should figure out that
you were probably showing the ace of spades, not a real spade suit. Your two
bids describe the two most pertinent features of your hand—the spade ace and
trump support. (The diamonds are not worth writing home about.)

2. ♠ K Q 10 8 5 2   ♡ 4 3   ◊ Q 6 4   ♣ 5 3
Partner opens with two hearts.
Bid two spades. When you rebid the spades on the next round, it tells partner
you have a good spade suit, but not necessarily the ace.

These two examples are very instructive. Responder does not know
whether the spade *ace* or the spade *suit* is needed by partner to make a
slam; all responder can do is describe his hand and let the opener place
the contract or solicit further information. But responder has the means to
show which kind of hand he has, and this is surely an advantage. The
natural response lets you have your cake and eat it, too. If partner has any
doubts, he can always check up with Blackwood or Gerber.

KNOW THY PARTNER

If your partner prefers "Aces Over Two-Bids," do it his way. It is better
to play a slightly inferior method in superior fashion than to louse up the
better method. Besides, here is a wonderful opportunity to improve partner's morale by going along with him.

THE JUMP SHIFT

A jump bid in a new suit in response to partner's opening one-bid in a
suit is another signal that slam may be in the offing. As every beginner
knows, this is a forcing bid not for just one round but until game is reached.
Whenever you feel bullish enough to *insist* on game, even opposite a dead
minimum, and are willing to crowd the bidding by jumping, you must have
some interest in a slam if partner has anything over a dead minimum.

This bid promises opening-bid strength plus something extra—a good
fit with partner's suit, a powerful independent suit, or overwhelming high-
card strength.

It is also possible to force to game or slam gradually, without ever jumping. When responder bids a new suit it is a one-round force on partner.

If you have two suits to show, you can force for two rounds, and you should be at game level when you are through.

With a good hand, how do you decide whether to make the immediate jump shift or to go slowly? Your major consideration is convenience in the ensuing bidding. Although the jump shift simplifies the bidding on many hands, it causes difficulty in others by consuming an extra round.

If no suit fit is immediately apparent, it is generally better to start with the simple, non-jump, suit take-out. If you have two suits to show, this method quickly suggests itself since you have two forcing bids immediately available. (Sometimes you have to "manufacture" a second suit for this purpose.) Also, it pays to go slowly when you want to show your distribution as well as your strength.

Perhaps the greatest value of the jump shift is that it lets you suggest slam without getting past the game level. This is most important in slam bidding. Five of a major suit is the never-never land of bridge; you can't help feeling sheepish if you voluntarily get up to five hearts or five spades only to be set one trick. If you bid six and go down, you have the satisfaction of a shot at the slam bonus. If you bid four spades and go down, you've at least made a gallant try for game. But since there's no premium for succeeding at the five-level, it is just plain silly to go down at five spades.

Partner opens with one spade, right-hand opponent passes, in each of the following eight hands:

1. ♠ K 10 5 4   ♡ 3   ◇ A K J 7 4 2   ♣ K 5
Bid three diamonds. Game is certain and slam is likely. If you bid only two diamonds, you will have to push all the way to the five-level to atone for your earlier underbid and to suggest the excellent slam possibilities.

2. ♠ 5 4   ♡ A K Q 9 7 6 5   ◇ K Q 3   ♣ 5
Bid three hearts, planning to make a minimum rebid in hearts over partner's rebid. An alternative is to bid two hearts and then jump to four hearts over the expected two-spade rebid. But this sequence might cost you a slam.

3. ♠ Q J 3   ♡ A Q J 7 4 2   ◇ A 5 2   ♣ K
Bid three hearts. Game is certain in either spades or hearts, and slam is a good possibility. The situation is similar to Hand 1.

4. ♠ Q J 5 4 2   ♡ 4   ◇ K J   ♣ A K 4 3 2
Bid three clubs, and then support spades. There is no need to keep the bidding low on this holding.

76

5. ♠ K J 8 6 4 2   ♡ 7   ◊ A 5 2   ♣ A K 3

Bid three clubs or three diamonds. The jump is a must as the start of an exploration for six or seven, and you have to manufacture a suit for the purpose.

6. ♠ 4   ♡ A K J 4 2   ◊ K J   ♣ A J 7 3 2

Bid two hearts, and follow with a minimum rebid in clubs. Game is a must,
but you do not know where. A slam is on only if a suit fit is found, and you need
to conserve bidding rounds to search for the fit and the eventual best spot for
the hand. By the time you have bid both your suits, partner will have made
three bids, and you will have enough information to know how to proceed.

7. ♠ 10 9 4   ♡ A 5   ◊ A Q 2   ♣ A K 7 6 2

Bid three clubs. Even though you have no strong fit or independent suit, you
have too many key cards not to put partner on immediate notice.

8. ♠ Q 9 5   ♡ 4   ◊ A J 10 4   ♣ A K 7 6 3

Bid two clubs, and show your diamonds next. There may easily be a slam in
the combined holdings, but unless partner is quite strong, you'll need to find
the very best spot to bring it home. It is important to paint an accurate picture
of your hand, and you cannot afford to throw out a bidding round with an
immediate jump. At your third turn you should plan to emerge with spade
support. By the time you are through with this slow-moving but powerful
series of bids, partner will know your strength and distribution right down to
your singleton heart.

Sometimes when you jump-shift, you are hell-bent for slam, no matter
how minimum partner's opener may be. Other times you have had your
say with your first jump and leave further slam action up to partner.
Strangely, many players don't know when to let well enough alone:

♠ 6 4   ♡ K Q 9 6   ◊ 5 2   ♣ A K Q J 4

Over partner's one heart they find the obvious three-club bid. But when
partner responds with a mere three hearts, they cannot content themselves with a simple raise to four. Instead, they resort to Blackwood, rebid
the clubs, or venture to five hearts. If they end up in a makable contract,
it is pure accident. Once you make a jump shift on this hand, it is enough
to support the hearts. There is no slam unless partner has extra values,
and if he has, it's up to him to take further action.

THE DOUBLE RAISE

Many a slam is started on its way by an immediate jump in opener's major suit. If opener has definite extra values of his own, he is encouraged to probe for slam. Any bid he makes other than three notrump or four of the agreed suit is a constructive step toward slam, as shown by the following examples. In each case your opening one spade has been raised to three by partner:

1. ♠ K Q J 5   ♡ K 10 2   ◇ A 9 8 3   ♣ 7 5
Bid four spades. No chance for slam here, so just bid your game and have done.

2. ♠ K Q J 8 3   ♡ K J 10   ◇ A 10 7 3   ♣ 6
Bid four diamonds. This shows either the diamond suit or the diamond ace, and in any event a mild interest in slam. You don't have enough over an opener to get really enthusiastio, but it's worth one try. The rest of the job of getting to slam is partner's. Even if he bids four hearts, showing the ace and expressing slam interest, don't rise to the bait. Instead, just bid four spades. (This illustrates how both partners can make a tentative slam try without getting *past* the game level.) If partner makes a second slam try, at the five level—with five clubs, five diamonds, or five spades—accept the invitation and bid the slam. But perhaps your four-diamond bid is all he needs to bid six spades by himself.

3. ♠ A Q J 7 4   ♡ K Q 5   ◇ A J 9 3   ♣ 4
Bid four diamonds. This time you have a good deal more than an opener, so you'll go straight to slam if partner encourages you with either a four-heart or five-club bid (the second is the more encouraging, since it takes you past the game level). Even if partner meekly returns to four spades, you still haven't shot your bolt; you should make one more try by bidding five spades. As a rule you avoid bidding five of your agreed major, but here it is ten to one that the five-level is safe. If partner now can dig down a little and find some slight additional plus value, such as a diamond fit, he should bid six, secure in the knowledge you have a good play for it. It is inconceivable that partner would bid again without one of the missing aces.

4. ♠ A J 8 4 2   ♡ 5   ◇ A Q 10 4 2   ♣ A 4
Bid six spades. It must be either an absolute laydown or, at the very worst, dependent on a finesse or break. Don't help the opening leader by fooling around with any intermediate bid. As for a grand slam, it might be there, but you'll never know. You have to find partner with the king-queen of spades, the heart ace, the diamond king (or singleton), and one other king to make a grand slam. And there just isn't enough bidding room to find out if he has every last one of these ingredients.

PROMOTING YOUR HAND

Sometimes you hold a puny array of cards, but a strong series of bids by partner enables you to revalue your hand upward and conclude that you have exactly what is needed for slam. The two examples that follow illustrate this principle:

1. ♠ K 10 6 5 3 2   ♡ A 4   ◇ 9 7 3   ♣ J 2

NORTH	SOUTH
1♣	1♠
2♡	2♠
4♠	?

Bid six spades or at least five, if you know your partner is an overbidder. Your first two bids were more or less forced, but partner's jump in spades makes his hand an open book. He has promised a very strong hand, with five clubs, four hearts, at least three good spades, and therefore no more than one diamond. (It is axiomatic that when a player bids three suits in a sequence that includes a reverse and a jump, he promises a singleton or void in the fourth suit.) Slam should be odds on, for partner has no reason to expect you to hold the sixth spade, the spade king (rather than, say, the queen), and the ace in his second suit. Your hand could hardly fit better.

Now take the same hand and switch the ace to diamonds. You can now bid only five diamonds, a slam try. Although you have the same strength, the diamond ace opposite partner's singleton is less valuable than the heart ace, which could solidify his suit. Therefore, you leave it up to partner whether to go to slam.

2. ♠ 10 5   ♡ K 5   ◇ A K J 9 6 3   ♣ Q 10 4

NORTH	SOUTH
1◇	1♡
2◇	3♠
3NT	5◇
?	

Bid six diamonds—automatic. Sure, partner is loaded for bear, but more than that, he has the right singleton—in clubs. And you have the right side king. (The spade king would be just as good, but the club king, opposite partner's singleton, would be a duplication of values.) Finally, you can be sure that partner has both major-suit aces; with only queen high in diamonds, he could not have the material for his bids without them. Bidding six diamonds is just good sound common sense, no genius required.

THE CUE-BID IN THE OPPONENT'S SUIT

♠ A K 8 6 4 3   ♡ None   ◇ K 7 6   ♣ K J 9 3

NORTH	EAST	SOUTH	WEST
1 ◇	1 ♡	?	

Bid one spade; second choice, two spades. The simple spade response may seem unimaginative, but it will elicit partner's natural response, which is just what you want. Since you have later forcing bids available, there is no need to jump at the first round. Later, if need be, you can find out more by making a minimum or jump bid in clubs. By this time you will have some pretty good answers to several key questions: Does partner have a spade fit? Are his diamonds rebiddable? Has he good clubs? Has he bid notrump to indicate that part of his values are in hearts and are duplication of your void? Now, if the answers to those questions are reasonably satisfactory, you still have the heart cue-bid in reserve to force out one last crumb of information. It is the sledge hammer he cannot ignore, and you will be happy you did not waste it earlier when gentler, subtler probing methods were available.

A reasonably safe generality may be made: The cue-bid as a slam try is rarely made on the early rounds; usually it is held until after game level has been reached.

Blackwood—Handle With Care

Perhaps you noticed in the previous chapter that we found our way into a number of good slams and kept out of some bad ones without ever invoking the familiar Blackwood Convention.

To the vast majority of bridge players, this is nothing less than heresy. A slam isn't really a slam unless somebody bids four notrump.

Well, friends, that is the bunk, and I am here to debunk. No one bid is so misused, abused, and overused as Blackwood. I am convinced that if Blackwood had never been introduced, the slam-bidding habits of the bridge public would be vastly superior to what they are.

Any convention that seems as simple and foolproof as Blackwood is bound to be overdone, particularly when 95 per cent of all bridge players use it. But that still does not explain why it is so consistently mangled.

The first reason is that it is not understood. Blackwood is not a slam-bidding system; it is merely an accessory that helps solve a specific and relatively infrequent situation. However, it is the only system the average player knows for bidding slams, and therefore he uses it en route to every slam.

There are psychological explanations as well. Blackwood gives some players a feeling of power; for the moment, they are captain of the bridge partnership. They can ask questions and get answers ("Two aces, sir") with no evasive backtalk. Furthermore, Blackwood is a habit. If a player knows he is going to bid six anyhow, he might just as well appear scientific about it. Or perhaps it helps pass the time. But no matter what the reason, Blackwood makes the practitioner forget how to *think* his way to a slam.

Enough philosophizing. Let's get down to specifics and put this convention in its proper perspective. Blackwood can reveal the number of aces (and kings) partner holds, nothing more. But aces are only a small part of a slam. You still need to determine the best suit in which to play the slam and that there are twelve tricks in the combined holding.

Blackwood doesn't even pretend to consider these elements. Worse yet, it often wastes a round or two of bidding urgently needed to investigate these matters. For that matter, Blackwood is not even the last word on the controls needed for a slam. It only *totals* your partner's aces; it does not *locate* them in the crucial suits. Many slams depend on *which* ace your partner holds, not how many. Nor can Blackwood uncover voids or singletons, which also control a suit most efficiently.

Before jumping into Blackwood, ask yourself these three questions:

1. Will four notrump be clearly read as a request for aces, not as a descriptive natural bid?
2. Will the responses to Blackwood enable you to singlehandedly place the contract at five, six, or seven? (Remember, the convention has made you captain and partner can give you only the count on his aces and kings, nothing more.)
3. Have you explored all possibilities for finding the very best suit (or notrump) and are you certain partner cannot help you further in this quest?

Use Blackwood only if you can honestly answer yes to all three questions. Otherwise, look for a more efficient bid. Here is a checklist of the most common pitfalls:

Stopping at five when you can make only four. I have cautioned against overbidding game in the previous chapter, so I won't beat this point to death here. But please keep it in mind.

Playing in the wrong suit because you cut your investigation short in order to use Blackwood. There are few bigger swings than going down one at six spades when six hearts would have been a laydown.

Giving aid and comfort to the enemy. You may not need to know the number of aces partner holds, but the information may be a great help to the opponents. The Blackwood response, like any artificial bid, is subject to an enemy double to ferret out that one killing opening lead. Even if there is no double, the opening leader makes the negative inference that partner is not anxious to have that suit opened.

What is your best action on these two hands?

1. ♠ Q J 7 5 2 ♡ A 3 ◇ A 5 2 ♣ 7 6 5

NORTH	SOUTH
1 ♣	1 ♠
3 ♠	?

Don't bid four notrump. Slam is a good possibility, but Blackwood is not the means. Why should partner's number of aces be of compelling importance? He surely holds one, and you can't be thinking in terms of a grand slam. The hand will make six spades if partner has a really good double raise, but only five if it is shaded. The issue is as simple as that, and the only logical step is to ask partner's advice. You can bid five spades and pass the ball back to him. Or you can bid four diamonds and then, over his expected four spades, try five hearts. He should get the picture: you have strength—probably aces—in the red suits, and are urging slam. You'd be surprised how rewarding it is to get partner into the act.

Blackwood would only beg the issue. *Partner could have only one ace, and still slam could be a laydown.* Conversely, he could have two and you could still have no play for slam. Possession of all four aces is by no means the open sesame to a successful small slam.

2. ♠ K Q 10 6 3   ♡ K Q 10   ◇ A K Q 3   ♣ 4

You open with one spade; partner jumps you to three spades.

Bid four notrump. This hand was practically invented for the Blackwood Convention, and the convention for it. Partner must have at least one ace. Otherwise, how could he have jumped when you have so many kings and queens? If he has just one ace, you stop safely at five spades. If he has two, six spades is money in the bank. Give him three bare aces, nothing else, and you wrap up seven spades. Note how well the checklist of three questions serves you on this hand.

Here is a full deal from a rubber game:

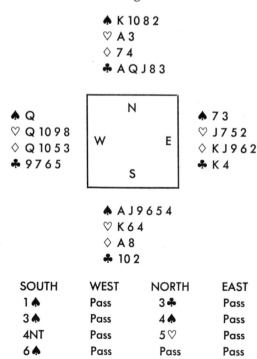

```
              ♠ K 10 8 2
              ♡ A 3
              ◇ 7 4
              ♣ A Q J 8 3
                     N
♠ Q                          ♠ 7 3
♡ Q 10 9 8                    ♡ J 7 5 2
◇ Q 10 5 3     W       E      ◇ K J 9 6 2
♣ 9 7 6 5                     ♣ K 4
                     S
              ♠ A J 9 6 5 4
              ♡ K 6 4
              ◇ A 8
              ♣ 10 2
```

SOUTH	WEST	NORTH	EAST
1♠	Pass	3♣	Pass
3♠	Pass	4♠	Pass
4NT	Pass	5♡	Pass
6♠	Pass	Pass	Pass

South would have been wiser to simply bid six spades at his third turn. The Blackwood bid was pointless: even after partner showed two aces, South could not bid seven, and as it turned out, the Blackwood bid ruined his chances for six.

Most West players would lead from the more solid red suit, in this case, hearts. But West was a thinker and knew his partner had a head on his shoulders. West mused that his partner's failure to double the five-heart response was most illuminating, and this tilted the scales toward the diamond lead. Since the club finesse was offside, this lead set the contract.

Bad luck? Maybe, but I'd bet on a heart lead if South had bid the slam without Blackwood. Also, note that if the Blackwood response had been five diamonds, East would have *doubled* for the lead.

KNOW THY PARTNER

You are probably just as well off if you cut a strange partner who doesn't use Blackwood. And you might even gain on balance. But, of course, go along with a partner who plays the convention; just mention you use it sparingly and only in clear-cut situations, and doesn't he?

There is no point in detailing here when four notrump is Blackwood and when it is not. There is seldom time to discuss this thoroughly with a new partner at the table, and, after all, it is the way he plays that counts. A simple way of solving the problem with a poor partner is to agree to treat all four-notrump bids as Blackwood. With a partner of known discrimination, the general rule is that four notrump is a natural raise if notrump has been bid previously.

GERBER

The same general observations on Blackwood are true for Gerber, only more so. In Gerber, four clubs is the asking bid for aces, but one is even less sure which way partner intends a four-club bid to be read.

I suggest you gently refuse to play Gerber, unless threatened, and then only immediately after an opening one- or two-notrump bid or first-round jump response in notrump. Here it at least serves a useful purpose, because a four-notrump bid would be a natural bid and you might occasionally need to find out about aces.

But insist that only a *jump* to four clubs be construed as Gerber. After an opening three-notrump bid, a four-club response is probably better played as Stayman, not Gerber.

Pre-emptive and Weak Bids

In the long run, the oft-cited law of averages provides you with your share of decent cards. Most hands contain something of value; many contain just the right material to make a little mischief.

Mischief comes in various packages. The gadgeteers have invented a bid for practically every weak hand; pretty soon the aficionado will never need to pass at all. In this chapter we run the gamut of weak bids, but as usual I decry most of the gadgets in favor of sound and simple bidding.

The mischief bid has many names—weak, pre-emptive, shut-out, nuisance—but only one purpose: to consume bidding space your opponents may need to explore for their best contract when you believe they hold the superior cards. The bid deceives no one. You serve notice that you have less than an opening bid with compensating playing strength massed in the bid suit. But even though your opponents know, they can't recover the lost bidding rounds to describe their hands.

Since it is exhilarating to bid and tiresome to pass, you may be tempted to stretch for some sort of nuisance bid on any excuse. But there are at least two good reasons for self-discipline.

First is the safety factor. A pre-emptive bid, like an overcall, should risk no more than the value of an opposing game. If the playing strength does not measure up to this, take a deep breath and pass.

Second, you have a partner and he, not the opponents, may have the powerful hand. If you pre-empt with anything from three to seven playing tricks, he cannot bid intelligently, and you may end up by having pre-empted yourself out of a game or into a big set.

OPENING THREE- AND FOUR-BIDS

The opening three- and four-bids are the oldest and probably the most effective pre-emptive bids known to bridgedom. Either bid guarantees a reasonably solid 6- to 8-card suit—at most, two probable losers—and very little or no side strength. The restriction on side strength spares partner a nasty guessing game each time you pre-empt.

If you have a suit that qualifies for a pre-empt, plus a trick or more on the side, don't pass; open with a one-bid. Your playing strength outweighs any deficiency in high-card points.

The higher the bid, the more effective the pre-empt. A good' bridge player at once bids as high as safety permits and then *holds his peace* unless prodded by partner. The initial pre-empt tells the full story. If a sacrifice is in order, it is up to the pre-emptor's partner.

The safety valve on pre-empts should be set at about 500 points, or the value of an enemy game. Non-vulnerable, bid three to three and a half tricks more than the expectation of your hand. Vulnerable, overbid by only two to two and a half tricks.

This safety factor dictates whether to open the hand at the three- or the four-level, or whether to open it at all. One exception: it is short-sighted to bid four in a solid minor suit. Partner needs only a fair collection of stoppers in the other suits for three notrump, so a four-bid serves only to pre-empt *you* out of this contract. Instead, prefer a three-bid or pass.

If partner has passed, the need for obstructive tactics is more apparent, and the risk of your missing a game is almost nil. As a result, some players relax the upper and lower requirements for a pre-empt in this situation.

Let's look at a few typical pre-emptive hands:

1. ♠ K Q J 10 9 6   ♡ 7 6 5 2   ◇ 8 4   ♣ 9
You are dealer, not vulnerable.
Bid three spades. A slight stretch with only 5 winners, but the 4-card heart length and minor-suit shortness are worth a little extra.

2. ♠ K Q J 10 7 6 5 4   ♡ None   ◇ J 10 9 8   ♣ 7
You are dealer, vulnerable.
Bid four spades. The arithmetic: 7 spade winners plus 1 diamond winner – 2 short of your contract.

3. ♠ A Q J 10 6 4 3   ♡ 4   ◇ K Q J   ♣ Q 5
You are third hand after two passes (the vulnerability is immaterial).
Bid four spades. It is unusual to pre-empt with both a good suit and side strength, but here it is good strategy on two counts: 1. you don't need much from partner to bring in the game, and 2. the opponents may find a lay-down game at hearts unless you obstruct their communications. In first or second position, it would be unthinkable to pre-empt — even at the four-level — with

such a good hand, because partner would never credit you with so much outside strength. As a result you might shut your side out of a slam.

4. ♠ None   ♡ 4 2   ◊ 9 8 7 3   ♣ Q J 10 9 8 6 5
You are dealer; the opponents are vulnerable.
Pass. The "book" bid is three clubs, but let's look ahead. There are 37 high-card points outstanding, and your opponents probably have a game, maybe a slam. A mere three-club bid certainly would not keep them out, but it would tip them off to your unbalanced distribution and place the missing honors in your partner's hand. Thus, if they landed in the right contract, they could hardly go wrong in the play. However, if you keep silent, declarer may guess wrong on the play of a close game or slam contract. In short, you concede the enemy an open road in the bidding in the hope they will crack up in the play.

RESPONDING TO A PRE-EMPTIVE BID

The pre-emptive bid is intended to hamstring the opponents, but it is ironical how often partner feels the pinch. Often he goes into an agonizing huddle, gazes at the ceiling, and proceeds to get busy at the wrong time or keep mum when he should be agitating. Sometimes he compromises with the "painful pass," which warns the opponents he has a good hand and keeps them out of trouble. Always he murmurs something about hating partners.

I diagnose his disease as "inadvertent bridge egomania." The symptoms are absorption in one's own hand, wishful thinking that partner holds more than the hand he has shown, and a pathetic disregard for the cards the opponents figure to hold.

Fortunately the cure for this malady is at hand:

1. Conjure up the "stock hand" shown by partner's bid.

2. Credit all other high cards and long suits to the opponents.

3. Decide what each side can reasonably make.

4. Take appropriate action.

The "stock hand" mentioned in Point 1 is the wonder drug of this cure. It spares you the mental torture of figuring all the possible hands partner could hold and then pondering which is most likely.

The stock hand consists of the long suit partner has bid headed by king-queen-jack, with equal distribution and no honors in the other three suits.

The long suit has one card more than the number of winners partner has indicated. A non-vulnerable three-spade bid evokes this stock hand:

♠ K Q J x x x x   ♡ x x   ◇ x x   ♣ x x

The same bid vulnerable adds one spade to the hand, since it promises an additional winner: .

♠ K Q J x x x x x   ♡ x   ◇ x x   ♣ x x

Of course, if *you* have a picture card in spades, you adjust the stock hand.

When you have pictured the stock hand, you see how it meshes with yours. It is immediately apparent how this line of reasoning keeps you out of mischief: You don't find yourself bidding three notrump without some spade help and good side-suit stoppers that include 2 Quick Tricks. You know your chances for a spade game are poor without three or four top tricks in the side suits. You are not tempted to bid some long broken suit opposite partner's low doubleton and lack of taking tricks.

But this is only the beginning. Your next step is to examine the opponents' treasure house. When you say to yourself, "We have junk," you also conclude, "But they are loaded." With a poor hand, it is apparent that an enemy game or slam is in the cards; if the vulnerability is right, you mentally congratulate partner on his bid and continue his good work by raising his suit. Because you would also raise to game on a good hand, you may even escape a double if the outstanding strength is split fairly evenly between the opponents. Each may credit you with the goodies his partner has. Down three at four spades—minus 150 points—and the opponents had a cold heart slam, vulnerable! One such hand does wonders for partnership morale.

An occasional hand requires delicate treatment. For that reason, a new-suit response to a pre-emptive bid is best played as a one-round force. Pre-emptor is expected to raise any major suit with three small cards; otherwise he rebids his suit. Additional urging may get him to disclose a preference for one of your suits, a second-round control (singleton), or, rarely, a side picture. But don't expect much information, because he hasn't got much.

The poet said one hand is worth a thousand injunctions, so let's proceed to examples. In each case, only the opponents are vulnerable.

PARTNER	OPPONENT	YOU
3♠	Pass	?

1. ♠ 5   ♡ Q 10 9 5   ◇ K Q 7 5   ♣ A J 5 3
Pass. You have good defensive values against any enemy game attempt, but no chance for your own game, at either spades or notrump.

2. ♠ 7 5 4   ♡ A 7   ◇ 6 4   ♣ Q J 10 7 5 4

Bid four spades. Your opponents surely have a game in one of the red suits, probably a slam, and you want to make it difficult for them to get together.

3. ♠ A 6   ♡ K J 5   ◇ Q J 7   ♣ A 10 7 5 4

Bid three notrump. It looks like seven spade tricks, one club, and — hopefully — one trick in a red suit. You don't try four spades, instead, because it is one trick higher and an opening lead through your red suits might cost you a trick. Besides, partner can always return to four spades if he doesn't have the stock hand.

4. ♠ 6 4   ♡ K J 9 6 3   ◇ A Q 7   ♣ A Q J

Bid four spades. You may easily produce the four tricks partner needs for this contract. Three notrump is a poor gamble, since you might be unable to get to dummy's spades. Don't even contemplate a slam after a pre-empt without 4 Quick Tricks, including two aces and second-round control in the third suit (even then you need 12 accessible winners and some assurance that partner has the trump ace *and* no trump loser).

THE WEAK JUMP OVERCALL

I don't consider the weak, or pre-emptive, jump overcall (touched on briefly in Chapter 8) a gadget. Perhaps *weak* is a misnomer, since the bid does announce definite values. However, the emphasis is on a playable suit and other distributional values rather than high-card strength. Unless partner has passed, the weak jump overcall generally indicates a hand that does not qualify for an opening one-bid.

Admittedly, the weak jump overcall deprives the opponents of only one round of bidding. But don't underestimate the value of a one-round pre-empt. Frequently you fix the opponents by either shutting them out of the bidding or exciting them into an overambitious contract. Moreover, the pre-empt has a cumulative effect on aggressive opponents; after a while they won't let you get away with your shut-out tactics, and as their over-bidding becomes more flagrant, your profits soar.

Even more important than the shut-out effect is the bid's description of a definite type of hand. This enables partner to know how far to go in competing for a part-score or sacrificing against a game. Think back to the times partner made a simple overcall and you were wary about raising with only two small cards despite a goodly smattering of other high cards. If partner had made a *jump* overcall, it would have told you he had a good suit and you could have made an immediate competitive raise.

And what about those "one-and-a-half-spade overcalls"—the kind that most people overcall one spade on and next time around would like to bid two spades on as a competitive maneuver, *if they had the chance.* In her fine book, *All The Tricks,* Helen Sobel wrote that she likes to bid two spades *immediately* in this situation. This tactic not only puts a crimp in the opponents' bidding style, but also alerts partner to the type of hand you hold so he can co-operate in competing. Furthermore, if the cards are stacked against you, the immediate two-spade bid runs considerably less risk of being doubled. If you only bid one spade, you allow the opponents to show strength to each other and then double you when you venture two spades on your second turn.

In the following hands, note the wide discrepancy in strength, as dictated by the four vulnerability situations. In each case there is an opening one-diamond bid on your right, and your recommended bid is two spades:

Only the opponents are vulnerable:
1. ♠ Q J 10 7 5 4   ♡ 7 5   ◇ 10 3   ♣ K 10 4
This is the low limit, both in distribution and in high cards.

Neither side is vulnerable:
2. ♠ Q J 10 7 5 4   ♡ 7 5   ◇ 3   ♣ K J 9 5
You need a shade more when competing against a non-vulnerable game.

Both sides vulnerable:
3. ♠ K Q J 9 7 3   ♡ 6 4   ◇ 8 5   ♣ K J 6
You cannot afford many liberties when you are vulnerable.

Only you are vulnerable:
4. ♠ K Q 10 9 6 5   ♡ K 5   ◇ 4   ♣ Q J 10 3
There is even less leeway in this vulnerability situation.

If your jump overcall has to be made at the *three*-level, a 7-card suit is usually necessary. As in an opening three-bid, the hand is unlikely to have high cards on the side. Not vulnerable, you might bid three diamonds over an opening one-spade bid with:

♠ J 5   ♡ 4   ◇ K J 10 9 7 4 3   ♣ Q J 6

If partner has passed, it may be good strategy to jump-overcall on a hand that qualifies for an opening one-bid:

♠ A J 10 8 5 3   ♡ 7 5   ◇ K 5   ♣ K 10 9
Pass — 1 diamond — ?

Bid two spades. Game for your side is remote after partner's pass. Your jump overcall lets partner know you have a good suit, so he can help compete for the part-score. He cannot suspect your high-card strength, but *neither can the opponents.* Thus your bid may excite them to the point of ruin. You have double-crossed them and have lost little or nothing by misleading partner. If he has a maximum hand with a good fit, he will raise for competitive purposes if for no other.

As noted previously, the *strong* jump overcall was formerly used for the rare enormous hand that pleaded for partner to respond on the slightest excuse. However you have other sequences to describe this type of hand. For example, your right-hand opponent opens with one club and you hold:

5. ♠ A K J 10 7 5 3   ♡ 4   ◇ A J 2   ♣ 7 5

Double, and then bid spades. If you bid two spades immediately, you may well miss out on a game-going hand. But won't the double encourage partner to bid hearts – opposite your singleton? Of course, but that is only a theoretical drawback. If he persists with hearts, your spades are good enough to keep overbidding him, and he should get the message in plenty of time.

Don't *force* just any partner to use the weak jump overcall. But if you conclude it is a good weapon, simply ask him not to disturb your jump overcalls without some concrete values. You can solemnly promise you'll treat his jump overcalls like powerhouse bids, for I am happy to predict they will practically never come up.

THE WEAK TWO-BID

The weak two-bid is a fairly modern development that works well with a knowing partner. I endorse it *for experienced and practiced partnerships only.*

Under this convention, two clubs is the only game-forcing bid, and opening bidder names his real suit later (more reason for needing a regular partner and a complete understanding). This leaves two diamonds, two hearts, and two spades available to portray a hand with a good 6-card suit and without the high-card values for a one-bid.

The weak two-bid is kissing kin to the weak jump overcall. Briefly it shows about 1 less Quick Trick than an opening one-bid. The safety factors and the effect of a passing partner are the same as for both the weak jump overcall and the opening three- (or four-) bid.

Some examples:

1. ♠ A J 10 8 5 2   ♡ 3   ◊ K 10 8 4   ♣ 7 6
Bid two spades, but pass if vulnerable against non-vulnerable opponents.

2. ♠ K Q 10 9 6 5   ♡ 7 4   ◊ Q 10 9   ♣ 6 3
Bid two spades. Pass if you are vulnerable.

3. ♠ A K J 10 7 4   ♡ J 3   ◊ Q J 8 5   ♣ 6
You are vulnerable, fourth hand after three passes.
Bid two spades. This paints a perfect picture. It tells partner you have: 1. the material for a one-bid (otherwise you'd pass the hand out), 2. a good 6-card spade suit, and 3. a shortage of high cards and therefore a desire to keep the opponents out.

There is some diversity of opinion about the best method of responding to a weak two-bid. Everyone agrees that a simple raise to three is preemptive and demands a pass from opener. Most players play any other bid as a one-round force; others consider two notrump the only forcing response. I have a slight preference for the latter treatment.

THE WEAK NOTRUMP

The weak notrump is generally either an 11-to-13- or a 12-to-14-point hand that is essentially balanced. Its users, of course, have to forgo the standard 15-to-18-point notrump, with all its advantages. I am going to dismiss the weak notrump rather summarily. It is a gadget designed chiefly for match-point duplicate play, and even then, in my opinion, has advantages only against weaker opponents. Furthermore, to employ it successfully in even those limited conditions, you must revise and reassess your entire bidding structure. I'll be darned if I'm going to tell you how.

THE WEAK JUMP RESPONSE

Roth-Stone devotees and other exotic system players employ a jump response in a new suit as a weak bid, but I can't see it at all. Partner's opening bid eliminates any real need for a pre-emptive bid, and besides, there is a greater need for a strong jump response to immediately announce a possible slam. (See Chapter 11.) Therefore, with apologies to its advocates, I give short shrift to still another weak gadget. I wouldn't use it with my favorite partner, much less a stranger.

THE UNUSUAL NOTRUMP

This gadget has caused a good deal of sound and fury—all, in my opinion, signifying very little.

Whenever earlier bidding makes it clear that a notrump overcall (usually at the two-level or higher) cannot have its natural meaning, it is used to ask partner to name his better minor suit. This bid tells him you are not interested in his major suit, and lays the groundwork for a possible minor-suit sacrifice.

The gadget is playable only after prolonged discussion with your partner about when a notrump bid is unusual and when it isn't. I recommend you forget the gadget entirely.

OTHER GADGETS

I have expressed my opinions elsewhere on most of the other tricky and artificial bids you may run up against. If I seem vehement at times, it is because I see gadgetry as a contagious disease that can cripple sensible bidding. (Look back to page 24 and note the many varieties of infections; be glad they're other people's problems and not yours.)

Bidding With a Part-Score

The skirmishing to convert a partial into a game or to stop the enemy from doing so is a crucial phase of rubber bridge. You might say it separates the men from the boys.

Here, a telling case can be made against the esoteric bidding systems. For most of these evolved from match-point play, where a part-score does not carry over to the next hand. But the New Scientists would have you believe their concoctions work wonders at *rubber* bridge, too. How can this be possible when these gadgets ignore the vital subject of part-scores?

THE FORGOTTEN PART-SCORE

The most common characteristic of a part-score is its tendency to be overlooked, even by seasoned rubber-bridge players. You can save thousands of points over the year by adopting this simple habit: look at the score *before* you pick up your hand and alert your partner when *either* side is on score. It is not ethical to draw attention to the score once you sort your hand or the bidding begins.

Say your delicate play brings in a two-spade contract and you chalk up a neat sixty points below the line. The next hand is being dealt out, and you notice your partner toying with his drink. This is just the time for a reminder about the part-score. Otherwise you may run into this dilemma:

You open one heart, and partner bids four hearts. He has leaped two tricks past game, so it is a strong slam suggestion—if he knows about the partial. Fortunately you have a minimum, so you pass without having to guess at partner's intentions. Dummy goes down, and, sure enough, partner has forgotten the score. But the hand breaks badly and you go down one.

Or you take his four-bid to six with a strong opener, and again it's down one. But it isn't safe to close your eyes and pass either, because *that* time your partner has noticed the score and you miss a small slam.

Sometimes, of course, you are protected. Your partner may follow the four-heart bid with a violent gasp or a hand-to-mouth reflex. Not very ethical, to be sure, but just as involuntary as his original overlooking of the score.

There is a great deal more to do about part-scores than just notice them. Because of the pesky things, you have to vary your bidding considerably, both offensively and defensively.

OPPONENTS' PART-SCORE

Defensively, restraint should be your watchword. It can be most annoying to sit idly by and watch the opponents score game via a measly two-spade contract; even the most conservative player wants to stick in some kind of nuisance bid before selling out. But this business of pushing the enemy can be sorely overdone.

Take the case of Ray B. He cornered me at the club bar with this gambit: "That so-and-so Smith threw me for 3600 points on a hand this afternoon." He went on to detail a complicated defensive play that had eluded Smith, whose lapse had allowed the opponents to make their one-notrump contract. I sympathized, but was impelled to ask Ray how one part-score could possibly cost 3600 points. "Why, he fixed me," retorted Ray indignantly. "I went for two 1100 sets and one 1400 number to save that rubber before we finally went out."

Maybe Ray can afford victories of this sort, but I believe in saving enough for cab fare home.

In sacrifice bidding, the knowing player picks his spots. When there is no partial, he may risk 500 points to stop an adverse game; he knows his chances for game on the next hand are just as good as the opponents'. But once the enemy has a part-score, he pulls in his horns; it is not worth that price when the opponents will still have their partial—and that much head-start toward game—on the next deal.

Obstructive tactics often pay off, provided you do not go too far afield. You can shade the requirements for an overcall or take-out double by a couple of points, but anything beyond that is courting disaster.

It's the hogs that get hurt. Be content to boost the opponents one or two levels beyond game. One partner should do the pushing, while the other sits back or, at most, offers a mild assist. The huge set results when both partners get busy at the same time. Remember, the part-score will still be there to haunt you on the next hand.

Beware of doubling the opponents just *because* you have pushed them past game. Your partner may have bid the pips off *both* your hands, and it is not sporting for you to punish him for trying after the adversaries have let him off scot-free.

With the opponents on score, the best time to stretch is when you have a near-game of your own. This is a positive measure, at least, since if you bid and make your doubtful game, you erase the enemy's part-score advantage. If you go down, the most you have thrown away is your own part-score, which would only have put you equal with your adversaries.

YOUR PART-SCORE

Now let's proceed to a more pleasant situation: you have the partial, not the opponents. Since one or two rounds of bidding will put you out, you don't have room for exploratory bids and delicate approaches. Therefore, each bid should mean exactly what it says. The opening bid on a short minor suit is definitely *verboten;* partner may be strapped for a bid in a competitive auction and may have to raise with less trump support than usual. If he has to allow for your holding a 3-card or even a poor 4-card suit, he may have to pass and permit the other team to steal the hand.

Any suit you bid should be playable opposite three small cards. Lacking such a suit, you can usually open one notrump. Ordinarily, an opening notrump requires 15 to 18 points, but when you have a partial it may range from 14 to 19 points. This is a logical expansion, since you do not need the precision of the narrower range when you plan to stop at the two-level. However, you do want to play at the best suit contract. The notrump opening assures partner he can compete in any suit of his own and probably find you with at least 3-card support. (Partner can tell if there is no apparent suit fit and either pass or raise the notrump opening.) If, instead, you had to open such a hand in a shabby suit, partner might have to raise with skimpy support, and you could easily land at the wrong spot.

The notrump opening also cramps the opponents' style. They must step in at the two-level, knowing your partner can double any overcall more freely because he can count on you for something in every suit.

In short, the notrump opening gives you a better chance of both buying the hand and finding the best spot. It is equally effective when the opponents have the part-score and/or the better combined hands. It may shut them out entirely, or help your partner find a good sacrifice.

Everybody at the table has to allow for the possibility of your holding the maximum 19 points as well as the minimum 14. This causes more discomfort to the adversaries than to your partner. If he has a good hand, he can still explore for slam, albeit more gingerly. You, in turn, will encourage with 17 points or more, and put on the brakes with less.

SLAM BIDDING

Certainly, a part-score does complicate slam bidding. Without a part-score, many minimum forcing bids are available en route to game so that by the time game is reached a great deal is known about the combined hands. But with a part-score, almost any bid that completes the game can be suddenly dropped, and you do not venture past game without good reason.

With less room to explore for slam, you make use of several available countermeasures. First, when you suspect the makings of a slam, get in one low bid under the game level. This will elicit a natural response from partner, which will help guide you.

For example, if you have 60 on score and partner opens one heart, a one-spade response from you is forcing but does not crowd your partner. Or if you have a 40-point partial and partner opens one heart, you can bid two diamonds, two clubs, or one spade to get his normal rebid.

This tactic is useless when you have a part-score of 70 or 80 points; partner may pass any non-jump response, since game has already been reached. Therefore, you must make a jump bid if you have the necessary values.

The strongest slam try is a jump in a new suit. Without a part-score, this is forcing to game. With a part-score, it must be treated as an absolute force for one round. Thus, with 60 on score after partner opens one spade, three clubs is the best action in both these hands, with a spade raise held in reserve for the following round:

1. ♠ K J 10 5	♡ 4	◊ K 6	♣ A K J 9 3 2
2. ♠ Q 9 8 5 4 2	♡ 5	◊ K Q 4	♣ A K 3

There is just so much time for discussion before a new partnership is formed at the bridge table, and chances are part-score bidding won't be taken up. If partner is doubtful and you haven't discussed the matter, don't risk a jump in a short suit—as in Hand 2. He may leave you there with only three clubs, or even a doubleton, in support. Instead, leap to four spades.

Next to the jump shift, the most powerful bid is a *triple* jump, and *after* that a double jump. Both bids suggest a slam but are not forcing. Instead of memorizing specific requirements for these bids, just remember that neither of them should jeopardize the sure game. In other words, you need a hand that will bring home your contract even opposite a bare opener.

97

With a 60 part-score, opener makes a further bid on a one-spade—three-spade auction only if he has distinct additional values. But on the one-spade —four-spade sequence, he makes another bid on the slightest pretext. If opener hears an immediate *five*-spade response to his one-spade opener, he should go to slam on any sound opening bid.

With a partial of 70 or more, it would be helpful if a simple raise from one to two spades could be reserved as a mild slam try, since it takes the partnership past game. For example:

3. ♠ K J 8 2   ♡ 9 5   ◇ A Q 6 5   ♣ Q J 7

However, the single raise is also needed as a pre-emptive measure to keep the opponents from getting together when you hold a weak hand such as:

4. ♠ Q 8 6 5 2   ♡ 6   ◇ K 8 6 4   ♣ 7 6 3

The solution is to employ the single raise for *both* types of hands. Opener bids again only if he has considerably more than a minimum. If you raised with Hand 3, you can now take positive action, but with Hand 4 you pass any spade contract (or simply return to spades after a bid in a new suit).

If on Hand 3 partner passes your two-spade raise, you need feel no regrets; he would need a lot more than a minimum to bring in a slam. Whatever accuracy you give up by the ambiguous simple raise is offset by the fact that the opponents are equally in the dark and are kept off balance.

A *jump* response in notrump that goes past the game level is a slam try; therefore, it should have a built-in reserve. Like the double or triple raise in a suit, it should never endanger your sure game. Thus with a part-score of 70, a two-notrump response should show about the equivalent of a minimum *three*-notrump response without the part-score. Further, a bid of three notrump with a partial clearly shows more than the same bid without a partial. This safety margin eliminates the discouraging experience of going down at some high contract with high cards aplenty because there is an overlap and no long-suit tricks.

RESPONDING HAND

When on score, don't respond in a barely biddable suit—just as you wouldn't *open* such a suit. Your partner should feel safe in raising your suit with moderate trump support; he should not feel compelled to yank you out of your suit unless he has a very good one of his own. With 60 on score, and a one-spade bid by partner, prefer to respond one notrump with:

♠ 7 5   ♡ Q 8 7 5 2   ◇ A K 7   ♣ Q 8 6

rather than two hearts on that shabby heart holding. And raise to two spades with:

♠ J 6 4   ♡ A Q 6 5 3   ◇ Q J 7   ♣ 8 4

Similarly, you open one spade and partner responds two hearts:

♠ A K Q 4 2   ♡ 7 6   ◇ J 7 6 2   ♣ K 3

Pass. Don't rebid two spades. There is no slam. Partner has promised a decent heart suit and may have a singleton or void in spades. He surely has nothing like the two previous hands if he follows my advice.

Responder should try to prepare his future bidding with an eye to enemy interference. For example, with 40 on score, partner opens with one spade:

♠ K 8 6   ♡ 9 4 3   ◇ 7 5   ♣ A J 10 8 6

Without a part-score you'd rate this as a one-bid hand, and choose the more helpful spade raise. However, with a part-score you may want to bid twice if the other team tries to push you. How can you show your clubs and support spades without getting too high?

If you raise spades immediately and the next player comes in with three hearts or three diamonds, you face one of these sour choices: bidding four clubs, which raises the bidding level; raising spades a second time with only three trumps; or passing and possibly missing an easy game.

So you bid two clubs first, and then bid spades without increasing the bidding level if the opponents compete. Partner now knows you have at least five clubs and only three spades, information that should help him in bidding if the opponents persist. Furthermore, you can probably get your spade bid in at the two-level, since the other team's red-suit overcall will also be at the two-level.

MISFIT HANDS

When one side has a misfit, the other team usually has one, too. You can apply this observation when you have a part-score by means of reverse psychology: drop a suspected misfit hand as soon as game is reached. Explore no more. You may be in a poor contract, but your apparent satisfaction with your spot may encourage the other side to step in—perhaps in the very suit you were going to bid.

Perspective

The vocabulary of bidding totals fifteen words: clubs, diamonds, hearts, spades, no trump, one, two, three, four, five, six, seven, pass, double, redouble.

These can be combined into only thirty-eight acceptable expressions. (Some enterprising players get considerable extra mileage with variations in tone, pitch, and timing, but such ingenuity doesn't make friends.)

However, there are more than 635 billion possible bridge hands! How, then, can you possibly describe your hand to your partner?

Obviously, you cannot describe the *complete* hand. The most you can do is indicate the type and strength and a couple of the most important features. Even this is an impossible load for one bid. But a *sequence* of bids can convey a remarkably accurate picture of a hand. Each successive bid narrows down the possibilities of the hand you hold.

Once you view the bidding as a logical sequence instead of a series of unrelated messages, your whole game perks up. In large measure this is a matter of acquiring perspective.

THE "REVERSE" BID

The catch phrase "reverse bidding" takes the place of perspective in the minds of many bridge players. Rather than listen to the bidding and draw logical inferences from it, they automatically react, "Ah, that's a reverse bid; it shows strength."

A reverse is merely a sequence in which a lower-ranking suit is bid before a higher-ranking suit. Depending on the particular sequence, it may be based on a strong hand, a bare minimum, or anything in between. The unknown bridge teacher who coined the expression *reverse bidding* was undoubtedly trying to dramatize its implication of strength in *one particular* reverse sequence. Unfortunately the label stuck, and for two decades a goodly proportion of bridge players has believed *all* reverses promise strong hands.

Let me burst this little bubble right now. The essential fact is whether this non-jump bid forces the auction to an unnecessarily high level. If it does, then the opening bidder must have the necessary reserve strength; hence it is a strong sequence.

For example:

1.	OPENER	RESPONDER
	1♣	1♠
	2♡	

If responder prefers clubs to hearts (quite likely, since opener has shown longer clubs), he has to go to the three-level to show it. Since the one-spade response does not promise much, opener must have a good hand.

Another case:

2.	OPENER	RESPONDER
	1♡	1NT
	2♠	

Again the partnership will land at the three-level if responder prefers the first-bid suit, and again this is quite likely. Note that one notrump is a limited response; thus opener cannot even hope for a good hand opposite him. He himself must have the wherewithal.

I want to burst another bubble. As has been demonstrated, a true reverse may force the bidding up an extra level and is therefore logically a *strength-showing* bid. It is that and no more. It is not a *forcing* bid, as some players apparently believe. Thus, if you bid one club, partner bids one notrump, and spades is your other suit, bid *three* spades to be absolutely certain partner speaks again. Two spades would be a strong bid and somewhat of an urge; it *might* get him to bid again, but he has a definite right to pass.

You may wonder how opener bids a minimum two-suiter when he has more cards in the lower-ranking suit. In Sequence 1 he opens one club, but will rebid either two clubs or one notrump (over one spade), whichever better describes his hand. This does not jeopardize too much his chances of finding a good heart contract, because responder can still bid two hearts on his own with a decent hand. (If responder has a weak hand with a 4-card suit in both majors, he should have responded one heart in the first place.)

And in Sequence 2, opener would start with one spade, instead of one heart, on a hand like:

♠ K Q J 5   ♡ A Q 9 7 4   ◇ Q 2   ♣ 8 5

On the next round he would bid two hearts, offering his partner a choice

101

at the two-level. Partner may occasionally be deceived about the relative suit length, but will not be misled about the overall strength.

I had better stick in one example of a reverse that promises nothing over a bare opener; otherwise I haven't really done my job of bubble-bursting:

OPENER	RESPONDER
1 ♣	1 ♡
1 ♠	

Opener is forced to bid when responder names a new suit, but he chooses the cheapest bid available, and keeps the partnership below the one-notrump level. Certainly he does not extravagantly toss away a bidding level. All responder can count on is that partner has an opener and a spade suit and at least three clubs to an honor. To be sure, opener may have a pretty fair hand, but responder should not bank on it at this point.

An opposing overcall can sometimes cause a sticky situation:

NORTH	EAST	SOUTH	WEST
1 ♣	1 ♠	2 ◇	Pass
2 ♡			

The two-heart bid may sound strong, but actually is the cheapest available action after two diamonds. North, lacking a crystal ball, could not anticipate the overcall; perhaps he has a very poor opener and had planned to bid one heart over partner's anticipated one-diamond response (or one notrump over his one-spade response). If opener had been able to rebid at the one-level, it would have been obvious that his rebid was not a strong one. The overcall simply pushed the natural bidding one level higher, and there is no reason to credit North with more than a minimum.

The following sequence *promises strength* but is not a true reverse:

OPENER	RESPONDER
1 ♠	2 ♡
3 ◇	

While opener has bid his suits in normal order, he has bid up to the three-level on his own; *ergo,* he must have extra values over his opener. The only difference between this sequence and the strength-showing reverses given before is that in the latter, opener's rebid *forces partner* to a higher level to show a preference. Here opener does it by himself, and again should have the wherewithal.

Incidentally, in the best of bridge circles, this sequence is considered absolutely forcing on responder. Even if responder prefers diamonds, he is expected to scratch around and come up with another bid. The logic behind this is that now that *both* partners have indicated strength, it is unseemly for the bidding to die so suddenly.

One last tip: never reverse artificially just to show a good hand:

♠ A Q J 5 4   ♡ K Q J 8 6   ◇ A 5   ♣ 3

One spade is the natural opener, and the hand is strong enough to *jump* in hearts on the next round. If you, instead, bid your suits out of the normal order—starting with one heart—it will distort the distributional picture.

FORCING SITUATIONS

Several bids and bidding sequences have been defined as "game forces" —they commit both partners to keep the bidding going until game is reached or the opponents are doubled for penalties. These have been touched on previously, and are merely summarized here:

OPENER	Opener	Responder
1. An opening strong two-bid	2 ♡	
2. A jump rebid in a new suit	1 ♣	1 ◇
	2 ♡	

RESPONDER (if he has not passed previously)		
3. A jump response in a new suit	1 ♡	2 ♠
4. A jump to two notrump	1 ♡	2NT
5. A double raise in opener's major suit	1 ♡	3 ♡

These auctions are clear-cut and simple. The player who forces knows that the combined strength adds up to game and that the hands mesh—for play at either notrump or a suit. Thus, he must have a good hand with the likelihood of a probable fit somewhere.

In Sequences 1, 2, and 3, the player making the forcing bid is not only confident of game, but may be slamming. In brief, his hand is unlimited. Compare with the forcing bids in Sequences 4 and 5, which definitely limit the hand. In Sequence 4, two notrump is a pure point-count bid, denying the strength to bid *three* notrump or jump in a new suit. The jump raise in Sequence 5 reveals an inability to jump in another suit.

Innumerable hands do not qualify for an immediate game force but will produce game if partner has the right ingredients. On such a hand, a way must be found to *suggest* game and yet allow the hand to be dropped at some reasonable part-score if further exploration is negative.

The one-round force fills the bill, requiring partner to speak once more but not pushing him all the way to game. Its cornerstone: a change of suits by *responding hand* cannot be passed. Note that a change of suits by *opener* is *not forcing;* also, observe that if responder has previously passed, his bid in a new suit is not forcing.

This "change of suit" device permits responder to show two suits, suggest game, and still get out in time if there is a misfit or partner has a bare minimum.

In the following example each of South's first two bids requires an answer from the opening bidder:

1. NORTH	SOUTH	2. NORTH	SOUTH	3. NORTH	SOUTH
1♣	1♡	1♢	1♠	1♣	1♢
1♠	2♢	2♢	2♡	1♡	1♠

If opener's first rebid is one notrump, responder must either jump or make a reverse bid to force a further bid. A bid in a new but lower-ranking suit is not considered a force in this situation. Contrast these three sequences:

4. NORTH	SOUTH	5. NORTH	SOUTH	6. NORTH	SOUTH
1♢	1♠	1♢	1♠	1♢	1♡
1NT	2♡	1NT	3♡	1NT	2♠

In Sequence 4, North is free to pass if he prefers hearts to spades. The notrump bid indicates a balanced hand, so South knows there is at least a partial fit with one of his suits. With a reasonably strong hand, he should jump the bidding, as in Sequence 5. This is, of course, forcing. Sequence 6 is forcing on North, since South has bid his suits in reverse order; he need not consume an extra bidding round by jumping.

A *one-round* force is just that, nothing more. Some of the bright young men advocate all sorts of sequences that are "forcing forever." Partner never can get off the hook. I frown on such methods and document my case with the following examples:

NORTH	SOUTH
1♡	2♢
2♡	2♠
2NT	3♢

South's first two bids were both forcing on North, but North is now free to pass over three diamonds. This is a logical inference in light of the previous bidding. South might have a hand like:

♠ A Q 7 3   ♡ 5   ♢ K Q 10 7 6 3   ♣ 5 4

He certainly has the material for all his bids, and surely he has to take a fling at finding a spade fit at his second bid. But South should recognize that his partner may have been under considerable pressure in responding to both forces; as a matter of fact, North's bidding has shown no additional values over his opening bid. South should therefore be willing to permit North to pass over three diamonds if that's what his hand indicates.

If South had an appreciably stronger hand, he would avoid the non-forcing three-diamond bid. Stronger action not only would be available to him, but would stand out clearly. For example, if he had the queen of clubs instead of the five, he would have bid three notrump instead of three diamonds.

As responder, beware of blowing hot and cold in succession:

NORTH	SOUTH
1 ♡	2 ♣
2 ♡	2 ♠
3 ♢	

South not only has shown two suits but has reversed in the process. Now that North has belatedly shown his second suit, it would be a betrayal to drop him like a hot potato. After all, his three-diamond bid indicates some sign of life, and as a matter of logic must be considered forcing.

Here is a different situation:

NORTH	SOUTH
1 ♡	1 ♠
2 ♡	2NT
3 ♢	

First, observe that South's two-notrump bid was not forcing (it was not a new *suit*). North's reply does not indicate any additional values above those shown by his original opener. On the basis of the bids North has made and the ones he *might have made,* let us try to picture his hand: The two-heart rebid was a minimum and could have been passed. With a good hand, North might have jumped to three hearts or three diamonds at his second turn; even *two* diamonds would have been more encouraging than the heart rebid. So what can we conclude? Simply that North has an unbalanced hand, doesn't like notrump, and may be looking for a safe resting place. South shouldn't punish him for his good intentions by making a further notrump bid without some good reason—such as a couple of extra high-card points. And, on this bidding, two small cards is good enough support for a heart preference.

We have already seen that a jump to two notrump by a non-passed responder is forcing to game. The two-notrump bidder should not get cold feet just because opener rebids three of his suit:

NORTH	SOUTH
1 ♠	2NT
3 ♠	

The three-spade bid is definitely *not* a sign-off. Since the notrump jump assures that game will be reached, North need not do anything dramatic at this juncture. He may have a hand like:

♠ A K J 5 3   ♡ A 4 2   ◇ Q 7 6 5   ♣ 3

North, with his singleton club, is not exactly enamored of notrump. Still, he doesn't want to insist on a spade game unilaterally. His three-spade bid offers partner a choice.

Or North may have an even bigger hand and make the same bid. For example, he may be contemplating slam, and may first want to find out if South can now show some spade help.

A jump to two notrump by the *opening bidder* is a limited, point-count bid and not absolutely forcing:

NORTH	SOUTH
1 ♣	1 ♡
2NT	

North has indicated somewhere between 18 very good points and 21 poor ones. If South had to struggle to find his one-heart response, he can now drop the bidding. Otherwise he should proceed to game. Any bid *he* makes commits the North-South pair to a game contract. If he bids three hearts, for example, North must not pass. It would be illogical for North to suddenly retire short of game after making a strong bid and receiving a further bid from partner. Experience shows that South should have the privilege of going slowly to investigate whether game belongs in hearts or notrump. As in the previous sequence, there may even be thoughts of slam and the three-heart bid may be just the first probe.

RESPONSES TO FORCING BIDS

Whenever partner's new-suit response forces you to bid, you should choose the most descriptive, natural action. A change of suit does not imply additional values:

NORTH	SOUTH
1 ♠	3 ♣
3 ◇	

North was forced to speak again, and the diamond bid presumably was his most natural action. Note that if South's response had been *two* clubs, North would also be obliged to bid *two* diamonds, even on a minimum.

Now let us inspect this sequence:

NORTH	SOUTH
1 ♣	2NT
3 ♠	

Again, North's rebid promises nothing in high cards over his opening, even though it reverses suits and sounds powerful. North may have a near-minimum on which he intended to rebid one spade over the anticipated one-diamond or one-heart response. However, the three-spade bid does announce at least five clubs and four spades, and inferentially warns against notrump. North has suggested a suit contract and probably has a red singleton. Of course, North *may* have real power and be heading toward slam, but if so, his subsequent action will show it. It's wrong to read slam intentions into the bidding up to this point.

REOPENING THE BIDDING

The opponents' bidding sequences are also open for scrutiny. One of the most revealing is:

EAST	SOUTH	WEST	NORTH
1 ♡	Pass	Pass	?

The East-West bidding, or lack of it, may not warrant the label *sequence*, but it locates the enemy strength clearly enough. Your problem, as North, is whether to reopen, and if so, how.

The strength you need to reopen is dependent on your partner's proclivities. If he is timid or likes to sit back and trap the opponents, you can sometimes come in with as little as 6 or 7 points. But if he doubles or overcalls at the drop of a bid, don't venture forth with less than 10 points. Opposite an average or unknown partner, figure 8 or 9 points as the minimum for reopening.

When you come into the auction with these minimums, you are, in effect, helping partner bid his hand. This is risky business with some partners, for they may then bid their hand again—all on their own.

You have a truer picture than your partner had. Perhaps he has a fairly good hand and refrained from a borderline overcall for fear of West's possible action. You know what partner didn't—that West is out to lunch. Therefore it is sensible for you to protect partner. But don't coddle him. Assume that if he had an obvious overcall or take-out double, he would have made it.

The time to protect, or "balance," is when you suspect your partner has made a trap pass with a good hand and strength in the bid suit. If an opening bid of one heart has been passed around to you, your own heart holding often gives you a clue to whether partner has trapped. If you have three or four hearts, it is unlikely that both opening bidder *and* your partner also have heart length; thus partner has probably not trapped, but merely passed because he was not strong enough to come in. But if you have a singleton or even a doubleton in hearts, you can suspect a trap pass by partner. This is a classic example of a natural inference.

Let's translate this inference into action: you should reopen on the *minimums* given above only if you are short in the opponent's suit and can therefore hope partner has trapped with a good hand.

Aside from recognizing *when* to reopen, you must know *how*. The cardinal rule is to choose the most natural bid on minimum or near-minimum hands. (Let me point out again that a minimum hand for reopening is about 8 or 9 points.) Thus, when you are short in the opponent's suit and have no real suit of your own, a take-out double is the most descriptive bid; it is natural to ask partner to pick the spot.

With the opponent's suit well stopped and a balanced hand, you would lean to a one-notrump overcall. This would also imply shortness in the unbid major suit(s); otherwise you might have doubled. A balanced no-trump-type hand contains little, if any, distributional advantage, so it is hazardous to reopen with one notrump on less than 11 points. (But you might double or overcall in a suit with 8 or 9, relying more on suit length.)

In brief, neither a reopening notrump bid nor a take-out double requires anything like the strength needed for the same action in a direct overcalling position.

When you have a notrump-type hand of 16 points or more, double first and bid notrump later. You thus enable partner to distinguish this hand from the weak 11-to-15-pointer. Apply this same common-sense approach to overcalls. It would not do to make a simple reopening overcall after the sequence one heart—pass—pass on this hand:

♠ A K Q 9 5   ♡ A 10 4   ◇ 3   ♣ K 10 8 7

With 16 high-card points, you should double first and then bid spades. For still stronger hands, cue-bid the opponent's suit and follow this with a bid in your suit or notrump, whichever describes the hand better.

Another distinction must be made if you use weak jump overcalls. There is no longer a need to pre-empt, since the opponents have stopped bidding. Therefore the jump overcall becomes more forward-going and shows considerable strength above the minimum needed to reopen. For example, you would bid two spades on the last hand if the king of clubs were replaced by a low club. The hand is now too strong for a simple reopening overcall, but not strong enough to first double and then show the spades.

KNOW THY PARTNER

Although the theory of balancing is sound, it doesn't pay to go overboard. Some players have never heard of balancing and play you for a right fine hand if you come in. Their fallacious slogan is "Never disturb a one-bid." If you do, the next thing you know you are in game, doubled and without a prayer for your contract. At the other extreme are the players who rarely come in themselves and always expect you to balance. Such a player will not take you sky high, so play along with him a bit. But it is foolhardy to overindulge him when you have next to nothing.

FREE BIDS

A *free* response to partner's opening bid is defined as one made directly after an intervening overcall. If there is no overcall, responder tends to scratch around to keep the bidding open, in case partner has a very strong hand. But the overcall gives opener a second chance without responder's help. Thus a free response must indicate some concrete values; there is no other reason to bid at this juncture.

This principle is sound, but it has been stretched to the breaking point by many average players and advocates of fringe systems. They apparently do not recognize that you may *want* to bid on some middling hand even though you are not *obliged* to. A case in point:

♠ K 10 9 6 4   ♡ 10 6 2   ◇ K 7 3   ♣ 8 5
one club — one heart — ?
Bid one spade, just as if there were no overcall. If you keep quiet instead, you will have to guess whether to show your spades later. Why let the measly heart overcall prevent you from offering useful information at a low level?

Now take the same hand with the king of spades demoted to a low spade. Here the pass is proper, even though with no overcall you might have bid one spade. In a nutshell, if your bid would not have been a stretch *without* the overcall, it warrants a free bid *after* the overcall.

Test your perspective on a more advanced situation:

SOUTH	WEST	NORTH	EAST
1♠	2♡	2♠	3♡
3♠			

How would you read the three-spade bid? If *East had passed,* South's action would clearly be a game invitation. But since East has complicated matters by bidding, and the auction has become an intensely competitive affair, it is logical for South to want some say in fighting it out. North should be aware of this implication and not blindly assume that South is pushing for game.

Nonetheless, South's bid does indicate some additional values over his opener, or else he would have passed three hearts around to North. If there is any big stretching to be done, it is up to the last man to do it—in this case, North. South, therefore, can safely pass with a near-minimum and let North take care of the competition department. From all these inferences we arrive at a sensible evaluation of South's hand: He has more than a bare minimum, but not enough to bid game. Logically, then, North should go on to four spades *only* if he has a really maximum free raise.

Note one important corollary to this situation. Should South decide he hasn't the values to bid over three hearts, North may stretch to find a competing three-spade bid. It would then be a partnership felony of the worst sort for *South* to suddenly go on to four.

I think I've given the impression right along that I believe in being aggressive in the early bidding rounds. I do. (In bridge, as in boxing, landing the first blow is a considerable advantage.) How else can you determine in time which side has the better cards and whether your partnership has a suit fit? I won't risk my life savings on any one bid, but I'll take reasonable calculated risks to get my licks in early. Of course, if you cannot find security in some suit with partner, you go quietly; but you can afford to be venturesome when a fit is found.

Note how the two examples of free bids hold true to this approach. In the first, I recommended bidding at a low level on a none-too-robust hand. And in the second, an intelligent interpretation of the bidding lets the partnership compete freely without *pushing itself* into an unlikely game. As a matter of fact, let's change the term "free" bid to "competitive" bid, for competition is the life of trade—and winning bridge too.

Bridge abounds with inferences; all you have to do is tune in. Every time your partner (or the opponents) makes a bid, it carries some positive meaning. Likewise, every pass imparts a negative inference that limits the hand. The very fact that one bid was chosen over another tells you something. These inferences are even sharper when you subscribe to the aggressive-early-round approach; it is a tremendous aid to partner in figuring your maximum strength, and warns him away from disaster when he has a doubtful hand.

NO GUARANTEES

The drawing of *logical* inferences is the mark of a good bridge player. But expanding these inferences into a rigid systemic gadget is something else again. Consider the two-over-one response, such as two diamonds over partner's opening one heart. As we have shown, this logically shows a *reasonably* good hand—at least 10 high-card points. Nine times out of ten the holder of such a hand *wants* to make a second bid. Thus we have a meaningful bid that leads to a meaningful sequence.

But that is not rigid enough for the system makers; they would have responder *guarantee* another bid. At first blush, a certainty might appear better than a bet that's 90 per cent sure. But look what they pay for their guarantee: responder is hamstrung at his first turn. If his hand is not worth two bids, he is forced to respond one notrump—even with an unbalanced hand and a good suit. I am not convinced that this leads to smooth, descriptive bidding.

And when responder does produce a sacrosanct response at the two-level, what does that do to opening bidder? He knows a second bid by responder has been underwritten by the Bank of England, and so he makes some namby-pamby rebid, even if he knows game is on ice. Sure enough, the promised rebid now issues forth from partner, but it says nothing new since it was guaranteed. However, opener finally must come to life and perhaps hike up to the five-level (and go down?) to test for slam.

I just can't see the sense of concealing the full strength of one's hand until the last possible moment. Nor is there anything immoral in giving both partners some latitude.

"I Double"

"Double, double, toil and trouble;
Fire burn and partner bubble."

As alluring a feature as any in bridge is the business double. It is unfailingly interesting. It is a challenge, a defiance, and frequently a costly mistake. It is a glove striking a rival's face. (Drawing a finger across the throat to indicate a business double is poor as sportsmanship and wretched as comedy, but it does express a certain simple truth.)

Nothing else in bridge is so much a matter of temperament. It is like strong drink. Some players never touch it. Take, for example, the heroine of this true story, which dates back to when the late Hal Sims was at his most terrifying. Sims got to six spades in a duplicate game, with a little old lady at his left holding, among other securities, the ace-king of trump. She was content, however, to accept 50 points a trick for the set. At the end of the hand an onlooker asked her why she hadn't doubled. "Why, I wouldn't dare," she replied. "Mr. Sims redoubles at the drop of a hat!"

Business doubles are very important in contract if you prefer to win money rather than to lose it. The sensible approach is to calculate your defensive tricks accurately and to consider the strategies of the particular situation. The situations are numerous; the players who employ good strategy are few.

The weak and timid player seldom doubles. He knows that when he doubles a contract and it is made, additional points against him are set down in black and white right on the score pad. What he does not realize is that when he neglects to double and then beats a contract badly, he loses a bundle of points—even though they are not entered on the score pad.

The easiest definition of a *good* penalty double is one that yields 1400 points. The only trouble is that it crops up infrequently, and in the meantime a series of 300, 500, and 700 penalties may slip through your fingers. Therefore you must be a bit enterprising with your penalty doubles.

How often have you set a contract three or four tricks and then agreed with your partner that neither of you had a good double? And this may well have been completely true. But perspective in interpreting the opponents' bidding can help you spot *some* of these lucrative opportunities.

Ironically, the obvious doubles backfire the most frequently. When you double and have all the defensive strength, a skilled declarer can often read your hand like an open book. If there is a double finesse, throw-in, squeeze, or safety play that can make the hand, the double helps him find it. But when the strength is divided between the two defensive hands, a "diagnostic double" can cause terrific carnage. Now there is communication between the two hands and perhaps a cross-ruff; the defenders can each guard different suits against a squeeze; most important, declarer may play the doubler for all the strength and thus compound the disaster.

Most really lucrative penalties result from doubles of low-level overcalls. You have to catch the unwary light overcaller right then and there. He usually doesn't give you a second chance.

There is no such thing as a "free" double. This term is usually used to alibi a double made when the opponents are at game anyway. The double won't be on the house; one side or the other is going to pay off.

The indiscriminate doubler loses in the long run, and his opponents soon learn to redouble. At the opposite pole, the player who rarely doubles is played for a sucker by his opponents. A middle position is best.

I happily concede the platitude that if your opponents never make a doubled contract against you, you are not doubling enough. But when you double, have something concrete working for you. Don't double just because the opponents are at a high level. By now, they've probably exchanged enough information to know pretty well what's what.

It requires experience and judgment to diagnose doubles. Don't expect miracles overnight. If you are only a "summer-weekend" player, ignore all this advice. However, if you play frequently, you will get the knack of it. Just heed the opponents' bidding and build a picture of each hand as it unfolds.

LEAD-DIRECTING DOUBLES

Slam bidding has improved considerably over the years, and it is rare nowadays for a slam to be set more than one trick. You won't get rich quick by doubling slams for sizable penalties. But you can lose your shirt.

Let's look at the arithmetic: your vulnerable opponents bid six spades, and nothing daunted, you double. If you set them one trick (and you hardly ever get more), you pick up an extra 100 points. But what happens if they redouble and bring home the slam? They pick up 540 points below the line plus an extra 50 on top. In effect, you are giving odds of about 6 to 1 when you double a vulnerable slam (and even more if they are not vulnerable). It just can't be worth it.

Furthermore your double may help declarer to locate the high cards or anticipate a bad break. This is just what he needs to bring in an otherwise unmakable slam. Now you really lose a bundle.

Because of these disadvantages, the slam double some years ago acquired another and better use—finding the killing lead. Now the double helps defeat an odds-on slam, and furthermore discourages the useless kind of double just discussed. Originally called the "Lightner Slam Double" (after its leading proponent, Theodore Lightner), it is a significant improvement in defensive tactics.

The partner of the opening leader doubles to request an unnatural opening lead. For example, if the opponents bid a heart slam and the doubler has bid spades earlier, the double says, "Disregard my spade overcall; I don't want that suit led. Look at your own hand, review the bidding, and you'll find some clue to the lead I want."

Or suppose the final contract is six hearts with no adverse bidding and the opponents have bid clubs and diamonds along the way. The normal lead is the unbid suit, spades. So if partner doubles, he is clearly saying, "Don't lead spades."

The Lightner Double does not specify which suit should be led; it simply warns against the obvious lead. The opening leader can usually dope out the desired suit by looking at his own hand and reviewing the bidding. Frequently partner doubles because he has a void suit and wants to ruff; usually the opening leader has sufficient length in that suit to guide him to the desired lead.

Some bridge authorities interpret the slam double to demand a specific lead: dummy's first-bid suit. True enough, that is often the killing lead, but the opening leader would most likely find it even after the non-specific double. Opposite any partner of even fair judgment, I strongly prefer the broader interpretation, because it lets him find the devastating lead when it doesn't happen to be dummy's first-bid suit.

The Lightner Slam Double is not a plaything; you still run the risk of a redouble. Use the double only when the unnatural lead will give you a good chance to defeat the contract. Don't use the double if the lead you want is the natural one.

Lead-directing doubles are also effective against three-notrump con-

114

tracts. As a matter of fact, a notrump game is quite tempting; it is human nature for opponents (and us, I fear) to want to take a crack at eking out nine measly tricks and game, and to stretch to get there. A defender doubles if he feels he can bring in his suit before the opposition can collar nine tricks.

Here the lead-directing implications are more complex than in a slam contract. If only one defender has bid a suit, the double calls for a lead in that suit. If both defenders have overcalled, it is often difficult to decide which suit to lead; I usually lead partner's suit. It saves an unpleasant post-mortem, even if it doesn't work. If both defenders have overcalled and partner has supported your suit, then he must want your suit led. In general, try to milk all possible inferences from a careful review of the bidding.

If both of you have been silent and partner suddenly pops up with a double of three notrump, it surely requests a lead in one of dummy's suits; the logic here is similar to that of the slam double. If dummy has bid two suits, use your judgment. Usually, of course, partner wants you to lead dummy's shorter suit. But don't be wooden about this. Suppose dummy has first bid diamonds and then spades, and you hold A-J-9-3 in spades and 7-5 in diamonds. Lead the seven of diamonds, even though it is dummy's longer suit. Partner cannot be doubling on spades, since you have so much in the suit yourself. Be wary, though, of leading a suit dummy has *rebid;* declarer will likely have to tackle that one himself.

Train yourself to think in terms of bidding sequences, building up a mental picture of all the hands—your opponents' as well as your partner's. You will be amazed at the logical inferences you will draw and the considerable advantages they will give you. Also, you'll have more fun.

The Care and Feeding
of Partners

"A low-grade moron would have known my diamond lead was a single-ton. And yet, you dear partner, chose to return a spade."

"Partner, I'm fifty years old; I no longer need a nursemaid. Really, I knew what I was doing when I doubled."

"I have no one to blame but myself. No one forced me to sit down at this table and cut a character like you for a partner."

This sort of thing happens all the time. Dozens of bridge articles have appeared over the years with the same theme—"I Hate Partners" (I wrote one under this very title myself). Every bridge player goes through life a gory victim of the malfeasances and ineptitudes of his partners.

I am sympathetic. It takes all sorts of people to make up a bridge game, and you will run into your share of the characters catalogued in our Bridge Player's Rogues' Gallery (see Chapter 18). But I can assure you that the very expert who writes the sarcastic articles about his idiot partners is all sweetness and light when he sits down at the table with them. That is, if he is a winning expert.

Surprisingly, partners are people. They do not put forth their best efforts if they are constantly criticized and lectured. Of course, there was one major expert who didn't see it that way. He would treat his partner unmercifully, without the slightest concern over the damage to the man's morale and mental processes. His theory was that after the rubber was over, he would play two rubbers against the same party. We should add, however, that this expert had difficulty getting together a foursome.

Bridge players are largely a conceited lot; they pride themselves on their ability, whether or not they have any. (Can you recall anyone ever telling you that he plays a lousy game?) As a matter of fact, this self-confidence is a prerequisite for high-level bridge; it helps a player concentrate his full resources on the game and give his all in competition. In a very real sense, you have to *feel* you are a good bridge player in order to be one.

Aside from the beginner, nobody comes to the bridge table to be taught. Everybody is there to demonstrate his acquired skill by going away as big winner at the end of the session. If anything, each believes he should be the teacher—certainly not the pupil.

Therefore, one cardinal rule of partnership harmony is *don't teach your partner*. Not even if he makes the most elementary mistake. Perhaps he already knows he erred, but he won't thank you for pressing the point. And if he hasn't learned by now (after how many years of playing the game?), you certainly cannot set him straight in a few well-chosen sentences—

If your partner is a boob, better accept the fact silently. You can at least make him a relaxed boob, and get the best out of him that he has to offer. But needle him a bit, enumerate too many of his more flagrant offenses, and you rattle him out of what little bridge knowledge he happens to possess. Not only will he miscount trump again, but he may even revoke next time.

Some players bear the scathing post-mortem in silence, but no matter what the outward reaction, scolding bodes ill for the partnership. Mr. Milquetoast becomes afraid of his partner; he had enough to do concentrating on his cards, but now he worries about getting hell after every hand. He may try to make every bid of his conform to what you want—when he hasn't the slightest idea of what you want. At least, if you know your partner's blind spots, you can count on them. Once you lecture him, he may try to reform. Part of the time he will be successful, but the rest of the time he will revert to his old habits. And you will have no idea of knowing when he is doing what.

Or take the raging partner who bellows right back at you when you take issue with his play. Remember, he is your partner for the present, for whatever he is worth. If you fight with him, he may have it in for you, and then you'll be playing against *three* opponents.

Partnership rapport is not only essential, but surprisingly easy to attain. Just show your partner you want to work with him—not teach or criticize him. Keep silent when he makes an error, but make a mental note not to put a similar strain on him if the same situation recurs.

Give your partner credit when he comes up with a good play or bid. Take your share of the blame—and then some—after a bad result. This exemplary attitude is not recommended for its moral values, but simply as good partnership bridge. There will be monetary rewards for the rubber bridge player and more trophies and master points for the tournament player.

117

It may seem a superhuman effort to hold your tongue when partner has just thrown a bundle. But it can be done if you remember that your partner had some reason for what he did. It may not be a good reason, but he didn't know that at the time. If he had known better, there would have been no catastrophe, so there is no point in scolding him.

Of course, if the hand just played was a howling success, discuss it to your heart's content; this may annoy the opponents somewhat, but it cannot hurt partner's spirits. After a debacle, however, indulge in a post-mortem only if it will ease future bidding. If your side went wrong because a bid was mis-interpreted, you might be able to clear up that problem then and there. But it must be clear you are not pointing a finger because of the recent ca-tastrophe.

Some players—particularly in tournaments—are heard to utter the quaint remark, "I'll take a charge for that one." This may strike the bystander as juvenile—like the reverse of awarding gold stars for perfect school attend-ance. But there is real merit in the practice. If you're going to point out an error, let it be your own, so partner can go on to the next hand unperturbed about his share of blame for the disaster. Furthermore, your admission of error allows partner to unburden himself gracefully. The hallmark of a harmonious partnership is the honest admission of error by one partner and the gracious acceptance of the explanation by the other. Confession is good not only for the soul, but also for the partnership.

ADJUSTMENTS FOR PLAYING SKILL

You should make a mental note of the playing skills demonstrated by the different partners you play with. It is winning tactics to alter your bidding accordingly, though in moderation.

For example, take this business of trying to play every hand when you know partner plays his cards badly. It sounds logical enough, since you can probably coax a trick or two more out of a hand than he. But the maneuver-ing avails you nothing if you wind up in a contract two or three tricks in-ferior to the natural one he would play. He might manage to scramble home with *his* contract by dint of all his concentrated energies—or perhaps the hand is so easy that even he couldn't go astray. Most good bridge players are already aggressive bidders, relying on their dummy technique to see them through; if they press a bit more with a weak partner in order to become declarer, this may be the final straw.

However, when partner is notoriously weak at dummy play, you should make a subtle and mild effort to play more than your fair share of the hands.

Don't let partner catch you at it—it might destroy his morale. For example:

♠ 9 4   ♡ K 9 3   ◇ K J 7 2   ♣ A K Q 5

With a sub-standard partner, you may decide to bid one notrump first hand, despite the bad doubleton in spades. Partner cheerfully responds three hearts. Four hearts is certainly the best contract, but some players would persist with three notrump, preferring the inferior contract to the shame of laying this hand down as dummy and exposing the original lie. You don't have to go through all these gymnastics. Bid four hearts like a good citizen, but switch the king or queen of clubs to your spade suit before your cards hit the table. Somebody will notice the error before the play starts—if not, point it out in time yourself. Everybody misplaces a card now and then; it is no crime. And, of course, your original notrump now becomes an *unintentional* mistake. Chicanery, yes, but it will probably spare your partner's feelings. Furthermore, you can comfort yourself with the thought that you let partner play the hand—and at the proper contract.

The bidding methods recommended throughout this book tend to be successful with any partner, because they allow the greatest possible margin of error for the wayward partner. You cannot create a brand-new bidding system to play with a weak partner and another for an expert.

But in borderline cases your decision should play up — or down — to partner's ability. You choose the bid that has the greater chance of success with your *partner-of-the-moment.*

With a reliable partner, resolve the close ones by making the bid that allows the widest choice of a final contract. With a weak partner, make things as simple as possible; choose the second-best bid if the first choice might confuse him. Give up trying for the "perfect result," because your partner is only too likely to miss the gentle nuance of your bid and leave you in a miserable contract. Better to be content with a fair, safe—yes, even sub-standard—contract. (The same principles apply in defense: with an inexperienced player, signal with high cards frequently, even though this may aid declarer, too. Take charge of the defense by retaining the lead so you can make the proper shift yourself. With an expert partner, assume he is following the play as closely as you and share with him the responsibility for deciding the proper line of defense.) Take this case:

♠ Q J 9   ♡ A K 2   ◇ 8 5   ♣ A K 9 8 3

You open normally with one club, and partner's one-spade response is music to your ears. With the spade fit, partner needs little to produce a game.

A simple raise to two spades would be a decided underbid (unless you know partner is very aggressive). You have the values for a three-spade jump except for the required 4-card trump support. The right bid *opposite a capable partner* is two hearts, despite the fact you hold only three of the suit. Since this is a strength-showing reverse, chances are partner will find another bid, and you can then support the spades. If, by chance, you are passed out at an inferior two-heart contract, you can feel fairly certain you haven't missed a game. But—and this is the whole point—don't make the esoteric heart bid unless you know your partner is reliable and experienced. The average player would pass two hearts on many a hand that is cold for four spades. So prefer the second-best bid of three spades with a run-of-the-mill partner.

Here's an actual, subtler case:

♠ K 9 7 3   ♡ 10 7 2   ◇ 4   ♣ J 8 7 6 3

The bidding had been 1 ♡ — Pass — ? The holder of these cards elected to pass. This shocked a very good player who was kibitzing—particularly when six was made with a few breaks and gifts. In any event, four hearts was a laydown. The kibitzer was convinced the correct response was two hearts, and to prove his point, he canvassed half a dozen of New York's big bridge names.

No expert gave him a straightforward answer. Heads were scratched, noses wrinkled, and questions fired:

"Who was the heart bidder?"

"What's the vulnerability?"

"Who were the opponents?"

"Was it after cocktail time?"

After all the returns were in, the consensus was found to be that the hand was "too good" to pass *if* the opener was a sound, expert, or average partner. But with an overbidding and underplaying partner, most of the experts preferred a pass; game might be missed, but more likely a fat set would be avoided.

For the response to a sane partner, the vote was for a one-spade bid rather than a raise in hearts. This was deemed to be safer, providing better control against the future bidding getting out of hand. However, where only the opponents were vulnerable, two hearts was preferred for its pre-emptive value. (That was my contribution to the learned discussion.)

It was a close decision from among the three possible bids, and it may appear to be a case of hair-splitting over a prosaic hand. However, observe that none of the experts consulted gave a "book" answer; knowledge of partner and opponents, and vulnerability were the final determinants.

A Bridge Player's Rogues' Gallery

None of my readers will recognize himself in the parade of bridgeniks about to pass by. But we have all met them as partners, and will probably see them again. So it is essential that we review their sins, the better to cope with them. The first culprit to make the line-up I call:

THE GREAT SACRIFICER

He has a few scattered honors, a little in distribution, and deep down he knows it is not much of a hand. Ah, but that's before the opponents bid game. Now, his eyes light up and he blurts out his wondrous "save," for all the world like Sir Galahad. But what exactly has he saved?

It seems to me that most players overdo this sacrificing business. Some, like our hero, have a psychological compulsion for this sort of thing. But even saner heads are fuzzy on the mathematics of sacrificing.

Suppose the opponents bid a game, with both sides vulnerable. Everyone agrees it's worth 500 points to keep them from going out. If it appears that a sacrifice can be held to a two-trick set, most people take the save without further thought. What they overlook is that the guide figure of 500 points assumes the opponents have a *100% sure* game. But no one is infallible; even Willie Mays has been known to drop an easy fly ball. Of course, the opponents cannot very well foul up their contract if you don't give them a chance to play it. Perhaps the hand is unmakable due to a bad distributional break. It is even conceivable that the opponents have simply overbid.

So why deliberately throw away 500 points when there may be nothing to save? You stand to gain only a theoretical 100 points or so, but the bid could cost you a *concrete* 600. You could have entered 100 points on your side of the score simply by keeping quiet and letting the opponents go down, but now you have to put down a fat 500 on theirs.

Thus, in similar vein, there is no point in risking more than *200 points* if you have as good as one chance in four of beating the opponents. And if their game is a 50-50 proposition, it doesn't pay to sacrifice at all.

The Great Sacrificer doesn't want to know about such things; he enjoys playing the hand, no matter how horrendous the result. In fact, he's not content just to get away with his audacity; he wants more of the same. Let him force the opponents to the five-level over his sacrifice, and he's still not content—he'll top them again.

He can fly the flag with no assistance from you. Need I tell you to raise his defensive overcalls at your own peril?

THE TRAP BIDDER

This fellow acts as if he's out to fix his partner rather than the opponents. Here is a typical case:

The bidding:

MR. TRAP	HIS PARTNER
1♣	1♠
2NT	?

You are Mr. Trap's partner and hold:

♠ K Q 5 3   ♡ Q 10 2   ◇ 9 5 4   ♣ 10 6 2

Two notrump shows a good hand, implicitly begging you to go on to game on 7 points, so you oblige with three notrump. And the roof falls in. He now bids four notrump! (I once saw a fellow bid six notrump on the same sequence.)

Mr. Trap has some strange aversion to a mere game contract, it seems, for he just won't let a hand play there. His long-suffering partner has the choice of *passing to two notrump and missing game* or winding up at the four- (or six-) level and going down.

The four-notrump bid is an impossibility, whether it is intended as Blackwood or a push for slam. If partner really has such a big hand, he should find a better second-round bid than two notrump—either *three* notrump or a jump in a new suit. Then he won't need to go past game to show his power. And if he doesn't have such a big hand, what is he doing up at the four level?

Trap bids come in assorted shapes and sizes, but the technique is always the same: partner implores you to help him out, and when you do, he bashes your head in.

Here are a few more of Mr. Trap's masterpieces (sitting North):

NORTH	SOUTH
1 ◇	1 ♡
2 ♣	2 ◇
3NT	

Mr. Trap has come up with an impossible bidding sequence—a non-forcing rebid of two clubs, followed by a precipitous leap to three notrump. After all, South's two-diamond bid may just have meant he couldn't stand clubs. Perhaps the hand *should* play in three notrump; but, in that case, North's second bid should have been *three* clubs, not *two*. And, if the two-club bid were correct, nothing new has been added to make game a good bet.

East-West have a part-score:

NORTH	EAST	SOUTH	WEST
1 ♠	2 ♡	2 ♠	3 ♡
Pass!	Pass	3 ♠	Pass
4 ♠ !	Double	Pass	Pass
Pass			

Mr. Trap wouldn't compete over three hearts, bless him, but when his partner did it for him he punished him by going to game.

A variation on a familiar theme:

NORTH	EAST	SOUTH	WEST
1 ♡	1 ♠	Pass	Pass
4 ♡	Pass!	Pass	4 ♠ !
Double	Pass	Pass	Pass

(Mr. Trap has shifted to the West seat for this one.) Our friend had no way of knowing whether a sacrifice was in order, but he likes to take the bull by the horns. A simple two-spade bid at his first turn would have let his partner in on the secret of his spade fit and perhaps aided in the final decision. But Mr. Trap always goes it alone.

THE DOUBLATIC

Here we have a paranoiac type who has no control over his erratic behavior. When the opponents get higher than the four-level, he salivates like Pavlov's dog and the double comes out without conscious effort. There are many types—each with a distaste for counting defensive tricks.

The Temper Doubler: A hot-blooded type, sometimes labeled the "I-never-liked-the-guy-anyway" or the "vendetta" doubler. Playing opposite him is the most expensive indulgence in bridge—something like maintaining a yacht, but much less fun.

The Contempt Doubler: I have a case history on this one: He was sneering aimlessly when a little guy named Caspar came into the game. Caspar has eyes like window panes and apparently nothing behind. He has trouble dealing and rarely hits the table fifty-two times in succession. Our doublatic had endured two agonizing rubbers as his partner, and at last Caspar was officially his opponent. By this time Caspar had consumed three highballs, and consequently he bid six clubs all by himself. Now, it was obvious to everybody within three blocks that Caspar could never take twelve tricks, ever, no matter what he held. Our doublatic didn't even snicker, much less consult his hand, before doubling.

Caspar redoubled but this time even he couldn't find a way to lose a trick.

The Self-Respect Doubler: One of the less violent types. It takes this particular auction to trigger his reaction: The opponents stop at a tame part-score, he puts in a bid, and the next thing he knows they bid game against him. He must double to be consistent, mustn't he?

Le Doubleur d'Ennui: Similar to the Contempt Doubler, but motivated by boredom. Most often a keen player who gets roped into humdrum mama-papa games by his sister-in-law. As he dozes off, he hears a timid opponent quaver some bid or other, and doubles just to liven things up a bit.

The Hair-Trigger Doubler: Motivated by greed and one of the most dangerous of all. He is so far gone that he thinks he has a reason for his double. Here are two excerpts from a case history.

1. "I had to double, Doctor, when they bid six clubs; I had the queen-jack four times!" Declarer finessed all around him and made his contract. (At least he was on the right track. He would have beaten the contract—if he had kept his mouth shut.)

2. Some months later, on his way to a cure, the poor fellow held Q-J-10-9-8 of clubs against an opposing six-club contract. (Now, what had the doctor told him?—But this was different.) He's under sedation now; the opponents ran out of the double to six notrump and squeezed him for their twelfth trick.

THE VALIANT COMPETITOR

I can best describe the Valiant Competitor to you by means of a true story of one Charles R. In general, Charles played his cards very well, and he really did know the rudiments of bidding. On this particular hand he was my partner.

We had just scored the first game. On the next hand the opponents bid up to two hearts, unmolested. Charlie was the last bidder; he held something like five spades to the king-jack and a side king. Undaunted, he ventured two spades, was doubled, and despite the very reasonable dummy I put down, he went for 1100 points.

While the next hand was being dealt, Charlie's brow was furrowed by deep thought. He had said nothing. I said nothing. After all, Charlie was a nice fellow, it was only money anyway, and besides, with Charlie concentrating on an analysis as only he can, I couldn't have got through to him with a megaphone.

Just as I started to open the bidding, Charles snapped out of his reverie. "Sorry about that last hand, partner," he said. "If you lead a club and I shift to diamonds when I get in, we can beat their two hearts!" I was struck dumb. Charlie was too good a bridge player not to really know, deep down, that his apology was the *non sequitur* of all time. Even if two hearts had been a laydown, a *100*-point set in defense of the part-score would not have been a bargain. And as for 1100! But Charles—the gallant defender, the consistent taker of final aggressive action—felt he had been unfaithful to his bridge code only when he discovered two hearts could have been beaten. So, rather than get myself hopelessly involved in advanced psychiatry or metaphysics, I nodded pleasantly to Charlie's "apology" and went ahead with the new hand.

We repeat, Charlie is a good bridge player. But his heroics are purely emotional. The logical part of his brain ceases to function when he indulges himself in his little drama of fearing no opponent, no matter how well armed with aces and kings.

THE NOTRUMP FIEND

This fellow suffers from the delusion that three notrump is the only game contract and only he can play it. This malady is all too prevalent, and many afflicted players do not realize they have the germ.

It strikes a tender nerve, for notrump is the cheapest game available and therefore the most popular game contract. Whenever there is no major-suit fit, most partnerships look for a nine-trick notrump game in preference to an eleven-trick minor-suit game.

But the notrump fiend gets carried away. In his quest for three notrump, he refuses to support his partner's major suit. He opens one notrump whenever the mood seizes him, regardless of whether he has the proper shape and strength. Furthermore, he responds with leaps in notrump when a normal player would explore for suit contracts.

In this manner he crowds the bidding and misinforms his partner. He is blinded by the conviction that he plays notrump contracts brilliantly. It rarely occurs to him that with a trump fit a suit contract plays one or two tricks better because of dummy's ruffing power; he does not even see that a low trump can be an eventual stopper at a suit contract.

His most frequent transgressions: opening a notrump on a hand that is unbalanced or has weak stoppers in two suits, and refusal to show support for partner's suit. Here are a few other cases; in each case our culprit is South:

1. ♠ K 5 2   ♡ A J   ◇ K 7 5   ♣ A K J 7 6

The bidding:

SOUTH	NORTH
1♣	1♠
2NT	3♣
?	

Our boy blithely bids three notrump, ignoring partner's warning against notrump and desire for a suit contract. South's only intelligent bid at this point is three spades, which cannot be dropped in view of his previous strong bidding. It shows 3-card spade support, and gives North the option of choosing the final contract. Thus it is both a sound and a scientific bid. But our hero is only interested in playing three notrump. Why, if he bid three spades, his partner might bid four, and *he'd* be dummy!

2. ♠ K Q 6 5   ♡ A 8 3   ◇ Q 10 7 3   ♣ J 4

The bidding:

NORTH	SOUTH
1♣	?

One spade is the natural response; it tests for a major-suit fit before turning to notrump. (One diamond is a possible second choice since it keeps the way open for the major suits.) But our notrump fiend doesn't see it that way;

126

he bids two notrump right off, and partner with a balanced hand has no choice but to carry him to three. Partner may have four spades, in which case four spades is probably a better contract, but our single-minded friend shuts out that possibility.

3. ♠ K 10 6   ♡ Q 10 6 5   ◇ A J 5 3   ♣ Q 5

The bidding:

SOUTH	NORTH
Pass	1 ♣
?	

That's right, he's in two notrump again, even though partner may have opened a weak hand in third position. Two notrump may easily go down, losing the part-score. Worse still, there may be a game in one of the suits. A one-diamond (or one-heart) response would unearth the fit, but South doesn't think this way.

SIX-CARDITIS

An ailment common in weaker, overbidding players. A recent case:

♠ A J 9 6 5 4   ♡ A Q 3   ◇ Q 2   ♣ 6 4

He opens one spade and hears a two-club response from partner. Two spades is the normal rebid, since the hand isn't too far above a minimum. But our subject emerges with a leap to three spades. The 6-card suit has gone to his head.

DOUBLE FIVE-CARDITIS

This is a similar condition. This chap goes berserk any time he has two 5-card suits. I am particularly aware of this fellow, for "There but for the grace of God, go I." When I was learning bridge at the age of thirteen, a great-aunt uttered these immortal words: "Two five-card suits make the biggest hand in bridge." (That's exactly what she said, so help me.) Many players champion this thought; come hell or high water, they'll show their exact distribution—even though it takes them up to the four-level and partner is screaming misfit.

THE FORMER CHAMPION

This is perhaps the saddest story of all. This gentleman has been accustomed to playing in the most rarefied of circles, and has held his own there.

Now he has moved to a small town and can only get third-rate games. And he loses regularly! He knows more bridge than the rest of the players combined, but he can't seem to understand he is no longer playing with experts. He makes brilliant inferential bids at the drop of a card, but his partners never seem to catch the meaning. His side always gets to the wrong contract, and he doesn't know what's wrong. He's beginning to wonder if he's lost his knack.

Each of you probably has your own candidate or two for the Bridge Player's Rogues' Gallery. Fortunately for all of us we play *against* these culprits twice as often as with them. But be wary of that one rubber in three. You may have to sit by as a passive accomplice in their crimes, but you don't have to compound their felonies. Retire into your shell when necessary. It may hurt your pride, but it will help your pocketbook.

Some Partnership Calamities

This interlude is dedicated to the much maligned B.W.A. (Bridge Writers' Alliance). Despite the good counsel and conscientious efforts of its members, their readers complain they still have partner trouble. What better retort to these plaintive cries than to cite some truly horrendous crimes—all perpetrated by B.W.A. members in good standing.

Our first exhibit is described by eyewitnesses as the greatest upheaval since the San Francisco earthquake. North and South were (and you may have trouble believing this) two major sharks.

North-South vulnerable; East is dealer:

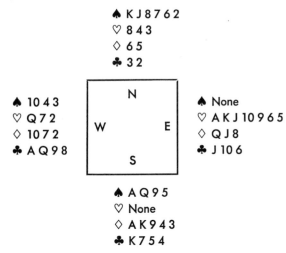

The bidding:

EAST	SOUTH	WEST	NORTH
4♡	4NT	Double	Pass
Pass	Redouble	Pass	Pass
Pass			

Mine not to alibi the North-South bidding. But since North and South were not noted for their philanthropy, they must have had some reasons, however obscure, for their actions.

By convention, South's four-notrump call asked North to name his best suit. When West doubled, North reasoned that his side might be in trouble already and it wouldn't do to show the highest-ranking spade suit if South happened to have an independent minor suit of his own. Since the double gave South another chance to speak, North decided to keep quiet and let South rescue himself.

South liked all three suits about equally well and wanted to force his partner to make the selection. Hence he redoubled, feeling certain his bid could not be misconstrued. But he had not reckoned on North's vivid imagination.

As best I could reconstruct it after sorting through the debris, North muttered to himself: "My charming partner could have taken out the double in a suit if he chose to. If he wants to play four notrump redoubled, I'm game. I can contribute six tricks in spades if he has a fit. So I'll pass and let him chalk up overtricks."

The pass was inexcusable in my opinion. The message of the redouble is clear, since the four-notrump bid didn't show a heart stopper. But even if North had some doubts about this interpretation, he still shouldn't have stubbornly taken the colossal gamble. True, five spades might easily go down, for all he knew, but surely no massacre was likely.

He, along with poor South, paid off colossally for his decision. West found the heart lead, and East rattled off seven tricks in the suit. The defense actually blew a trick when West amateurishly signaled with the nine of clubs; low diamond and spade discards would have sent the same message. When East berated his partner for letting declarer off with a 4000-point set instead of 4600, West's airy rejoinder was, "I didn't come here to kill anybody."

Don't waste too much pity on South. He should have foreseen that his buck-passing redouble was loaded with dynamite. It turned out to be too subtle for even an expert partner. I doubt you will want to try the same thing with a casual, unknown partner.

Ye of faint hearts and weak stomachs had better take a break now. Only the truly bloodthirsty can take these bridge disasters one right after the other. The following is to the Johnstown flood what the previous one was to the San Francisco earthquake. East-West up to this time were known as a top-flight team.

East-West vulnerable; South was dealer.

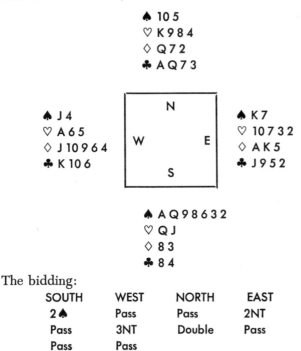

The bidding:

SOUTH	WEST	NORTH	EAST
2 ♠	Pass	Pass	2NT
Pass	3NT	Double	Pass
Pass	Pass		

South was using weak two-bids—to good advantage, I may add. However, most players would open three with South's hand; maybe South knew what lay ahead when he chose the offbeat two-bid instead.

East apparently got carried away. Like many other players, he assumed that an opponent's "weak" bid somehow made his own hand that much better. His decision to come in with two notrump was a *mis*calculated risk. West's raise was only a shade optimistic; he didn't know his partner very well.

The ridiculous contract was made worse by the unfortunate lay of the North-South cards plus a good opening lead by South—the heart queen. East won with the ace. Playing double-dummy, he could have finessed diamonds next and made three tricks in the suit, to go down only five tricks—a mere 1400 points. But, not unreasonably, he got to his hand with the diamond ace and tackled clubs, hoping to find South with the queen and North with one of the spade honors. Then the dam broke. Without breathing heavily, North and South collected seven spade tricks, two clubs, and two hearts—all the rest, to be concise. Down seven, or 2000 points.

Did you say overbidding partners don't frighten you?

For those who are still around I have one more disaster to report; it has come to be named after the Chicago Fire. The scene: a high-stake rubber-bridge game.

Both sides vulnerable; North was dealer.

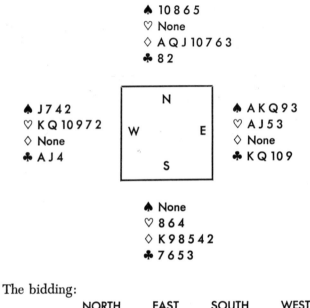

♠ 10 8 6 5
♡ None
◇ A Q J 10 7 6 3
♣ 8 2

♠ J 7 4 2
♡ K Q 10 9 7 2
◇ None
♣ A J 4

♠ A K Q 9 3
♡ A J 5 3
◇ None
♣ K Q 10 9

♠ None
♡ 8 6 4
◇ K 9 8 5 4 2
♣ 7 6 5 3

The bidding:

NORTH	EAST	SOUTH	WEST
3◇	Double	3♠	4♡
4♠	5♡	6◇	6♡
7◇	7♡	Pass	Pass
7♠	Double	Pass	Pass
Pass			

There is no misprint! South, with a void in spades, actually played seven spades doubled—and took nary a trick after West brightly opened a trump. Someone borrowed a slide rule and the score was computed—a near record: 3800 points. The only thing missing was a redouble; it would have brought about the highest possible score for a single hand. However, the opponents were not heard to complain.

How did it all happen? No one would fault North for his pre-emptive opening. With the huge East hand, I would have preferred the cue-bid of four diamonds to the take-out double—but then I wouldn't have collected 3800 points.

South's little brain had been churning away; the fake spade bid he dreamed up was a superb strategic move; it might talk the opponents out of a spade slam or get him a ruff on the opening lead if they bid a slam in hearts. But South was so absorbed in his own brilliant devices that he forgot about his partner.

The bidding went merrily on. West showed his hearts, and North unsuspectingly indicated spade "support" as a prelude for a sacrifice. East, well within himself, raised to five hearts, and South came out of hiding with diamond help. Little did he know that the bad seed he had planted would grow into a monstrous poisonous vine. West happily took the push to six hearts; he would have bid it anyway. North, being in that deep already, sacrificed at seven diamonds, and East, in turn, bid seven hearts, as he had expected to do all along.

When this came around to North, all he could see was that huge vulnerable grand-slam bonus glaring at him. Remembering South's bid, he took the bit in his teeth. Spades is the only suit that outranks hearts, so seven spades it became.

North should have suspected his partner's spade bid was a fake, particularly in view of the subsequent diamond raise. In addition, he might have reasoned that South could have taken the save at seven spades himself if he were so inclined; presumably South had heard North's earlier spade raise. But North was too far gone to figure out such things.

South might still have saved 3000 points—if he had been born a quarter-century earlier. In those days they were permitted to bid *eight* diamonds. But the rules have since been changed, and so South was just plain stuck with no place to go. (He brilliantly deduced that the opponents might also double seven notrump.) The crowning touch was that he had to play the hand.

So North-South paid out 3800 points instead of 2210.

Readers, take heart!

The Pre-Mortem

In Chapter 17 we mulled some principles for partner-maintenance. Then we sighted in on a few of the more heinous partners that wander into everybody's game. Last, we witnessed some shattering bridge monstrosities.

By this time you are probably wondering if there is any means to avoid being massacred, defiled, and thrown by that charming stranger across the table.

Indeed there is. I call it the *pre-mortem,* because it often eliminates the need for a post-mortem. It is a combination of selling yourself, interviewing your partner, and arriving at a working arrangement. As we shall see, the few minutes before the first hand are crucial ones.

Almost everybody plays bridge 1) to win, and 2) for fun, and in that order. Yet few players study their prospective partner and really get acquainted with him. With a regular partner, you gradually acquire the knowledge you need; but with a stranger, you must compress this learning process into a few short minutes.

What do you really know about him? Just because he holds his cards steady and wants to play bridge is no indication that he can. In no other sport is there such ignorance about your teammate. In sailing, for example, a skipper wouldn't dream of asking some stranger on the pier to crew for him in a big race; the man might not know port from starboard. In bridge, you may not get to pick your own teammate, and you may have to cut into a strange game—and an even stranger partner. (This is even more likely at a social gathering than at a bridge club.) That's all the more reason for you to find out what you can about this fellow who will play a vital role in your victories and defeats. That is, if you want more of the former than of the latter.

The first phase of a pre-mortem is selling yourself to your partner. Give him a big smile, so he feels sure you are looking forward to playing with him (although you may actually feel sick at the thought). That alone should produce a couple of hundred points in the rubber. It will also encourage partner to open up, and you can now proceed to size him up. Meanwhile he may be wondering how your bridge mechanism ticks, so be careful not to intimidate him. Don't tell him what a great player you are; just let your attitude show you are a reliable and worthy companion for his brand of brilliance.

Few partners reveal themselves willingly; each believes he plays a perfectly normal (albeit superior) game. I have yet to hear a new partner confide, "Partner, I overbid as responder, but am conservative in opening. I may raise on insufficient trump support, but I never try to hog a hand. However, I must warn you that an opponent's pre-empt sets my glands atingling."

A man's occupation may be some tip-off to his bridge game. You expect a stockmarket operator to be daring, an accountant to be precise. And if your partner is of the fair sex—well, that's a chapter in itself (Chapter 22).

Generalizations are dangerous, and a tentative appraisal is all you are looking for. There are too many deviations from the norm, and besides the evidence of the first few hands will soon be in to revise your estimate.

THE WORKING AGREEMENT

A working agreement between partners is usually conspicuous by its absence. A couple of vague questions and answering grunts supposedly determine the conventions they will play. Thereafter the only time either partner notices the other is when he glowers at him after some particularly blatant indiscretion.

To avoid this trap, set up a working arrangement with partner before play begins. Many players simply ask, "What do you like to play, partner?" Although this demonstrates a commendable desire to cooperate, it is a poor tactic. It opens up the floodgates to all the esoteric conventions this simple-looking soul has managed to cram into his cranium. Too late you realize they can only lead to trouble, and at some point, while he reels them off, you must draw the line. You can plead that you are ignorant of his latest gadget (which may easily be the case) or that you are just not up to it. This may get him to play down the middle with you and reserve his high life until he is your opponent. However, you may be forced to go along with his favorite concoction in order to preserve rapport. (It is downright cruel to ask your partner's wishes and then turn them *all* down cold.)

It's far better to take the initiative in suggesting the conventions, so you can keep them few and simple. Your questionnaire might go:

"Do you like Stayman?

"How about weak jump overcalls, partner?

"That about does it, I guess."

There is a good deal of psychology built into these questions. Note that you just name the convention—you don't explain it. Partner's reaction can be both surprising and revealing. For example, if his reply to the first question is, "Never met the gentleman," you know he is somewhat behind the times. He probably doesn't feel comfortable about point count either, so watch your notrump bidding. If he's never heard of weak jump overcalls, let it go; tell him you'll treat his as strong. (As for yourself, you'll probably abstain from them completely).

Be especially careful not to force *any* convention on a new partner. You are better off going along with his simpler mama-papa methods than trying to show him the superiority of yours.

The clues for judging partner are all about you. For example, the man who counts his cards before looking at them is probably a duplicate player; he may be ill at ease in part-score situations, although otherwise experienced. Then there's the quiet chap who plays deliberately with no rushing and a minimum of huddling: this is your lucky day, because he knows his way around. And—this seems almost too obvious, but so help me, it's true—the fellow who deals, and in general handles his cards awkwardly, usually plays just as awkwardly. Another clue to the duffer is that he sits bolt upright on the front of his chair (simultaneously showing his hand to the opponents).

OVERBIDDERS AND UNDERBIDDERS

After the first few hands you will probably know whether your partner is an overbidder or an underbidder. There are two ways of handling either ilk. The first is to compensate in the other direction to reach a proper balance. I can't help subscribing to this approach, but I restrict it to close decisions. If you allow partner's habits to distort every bid you make, your bidding becomes meaningless.

The second tactic was advanced by Ely Culbertson: "Overbid with overbidders and underbid with underbidders." Ely may have had the right idea. A certain class of overbidder is pretty shrewd at sizing up what is going on. If you are obviously putting on the brakes, he pushes even more to compensate, and you get in a real rat race. But if he senses you are right there with him all the way, he checks his impulses somewhat.

Now let's go back to the first theory and examine some typical situations:

The overbidder: In general, avoid making minimum opening bids and light forces, and take partner's forces with a grain of salt. However, keep in mind that some players push their cards by means of only one type of bid. For example, there is the addict of light take-out doubles. The tactic for him is to make minimum responses with even fair hands, until the honesty of the double is confirmed by a rebid. Another type is sound on opening bids but daring with overcalls. You can bid normally when he opens the bidding, but raise his overcalls only when you have a substantial amount of high cards.

The underbidder: If his overcalls are usually the equivalent of opening bids plus a good suit, treat them as such. If he will not give you a chance without being forced, make your jump bids on a little less strength than usual. If he is easily bluffed by the enemy's psychic tactics, make every effort to overcall and double in order to expose the possible psychic for him.

Here is one way you can do this. Suppose dealer has passed and you are second hand and hold a shade under an opening bid. Third hand happens to be a good player who is fond of psyching. Fourth hand, your partner, is ultra-timid; he believes everything the opponents do, and breathes a sigh of relief every time he can pass out a hand and get an even break on the score pad. By all means, open the bidding; it will give partner confidence in case third hand tries bluff tactics, and prevent partner from passing out a fair hand if third hand passes.

Occasionally such compensating tactics backfire into a sizable penalty. This happens when you overdo things a bit and discover, too late, that partner *really* has nothing this time. Take the full blame, because partner will never understand that he was basically at fault.

Your partner is an unknown quantity only if you let him remain so. If you want to win more (or lose less), you have to do more than glance at him and barely remember his name.

The Enemy

No, *enemy* is not another term for *partner*, though it may seem that way at times. Rather, I am referring to the two players at your right and left who have come to beat your brains out (and vice versa). I must relent in my dogged pursuit of the partnership concept, long enough to emphasize that bridge is a four-handed game—you are not just playing with partner; you are also playing against two opponents (the odds often seem even greater).

What is your attitude toward the enemy? Why, you are out to whomp them, of course, and have a fierce fighting spirit equal to the task. That's fine as far as it goes, but the resourceful player goes one better. He recognizes that the enemy can be right friendly at times, and he is happy to let them work for him.

As the opponents tell each other about their hands, they let you in on many of their secrets, and it is almost criminal not to take notice. Usually you can believe their bids, because most of the time they paint the most accurate picture of their hands that they can. It is losing tactics to be over-suspicious of the enemy's auction; unless there is strong evidence to the contrary, take their bids at face value.

You needn't be a trusting soul on every bid with every opponent. By all means, take into account that Joe on your left—as true and honest a friend as any man could want—loves to psyche you out of your shoes. The vulnerability situation tips you off as to when the enemy is most likely to be "operating." But by and large you should stick to the "Honest John" attitude.

You will still be fixed occasionally; sometimes the hands are so divided that an enemy's psychic goes undetected and you are talked out of a game or slam. And, in the nature of things, opposing pre-empts must take their toll. You might as well be philosophic about such occasional indignities. Congratulate the opponent on his bid and get on with the next hand.

Or maybe you would rather fight it, like our friend, Carl M. Carl has a psychopathic fear of being fooled. Once in a great while he smells out the opponents' dirty work, but oftener he takes heroic measures against a phantom psyche and has his head handed to him. Carl gets into trouble about three times as often as he unearths something.

One can reasonably accept a minus score as the result of an opponent's brilliant bid or play. But what can you say when you take a beating just because you refused to believe the enemy's bidding? Your partner will never appreciate your playing private eye. See how all this works in practice:

Both sides vulnerable; you are West and hold:

1. ♠ K J 10 8 7   ♡ 7 4 2   ◇ A 5   ♣ K 6 3

NORTH	EAST	SOUTH	WEST
1 ◇	Double	1 ♡	2 ♠
Pass	3 ♠	Pass	4 ◇
Pass	4 ♡	Pass	?

Bid four spades. From where you sit, a slam is not a good gamble. Consider all the evidence: one *vulnerable* opponent has opened the bidding, and over the take-out double, his partner found a bid, suspect though it may be. True, your partner's bidding has been encouraging, but not overwhelming; he did not, for example, jump right to four spades at his second turn. Furthermore, partner's four-heart bid may not be a slam try at all; it may merely show a heart suit and suggest an alternative contract. What else would he do with five good hearts and only 3-card spade support? For all he knows, South's heart bid over the double was a phony, and hearts may be the best spot for your side. Lastly, what about your own hand? It has no distributional advantages; on the contrary, it has a number of potential losers. And you have already offered one slam try. Putting all the pieces together, you should conclude that there is more danger of going down at five spades than of missing a slam.

Try this one:

North-South vulnerable; you are West and hold:

2. ♠ A 10 8 5 4   ♡ Q J 3   ◇ K 8 2   ♣ 7 5

NORTH	EAST	SOUTH	WEST
1 ♡	Double	Redouble	1 ♠
3 ♡	Pass	4 ♡	?

Pass. Here you must believe the vulnerable opponents and practically ignore your partner's non-vulnerable take-out double. East may have made a very light distributional double in an effort to talk the opponents out of something or to smoke out a sacrifice spot. Don't hang him for having tried, by doubling now. Declarer might then pick up your "natural" heart trick and the opponent might even have the gall to redouble and make an overtrick. As for bidding four spades, what gives you the idea that partner has a strong enough liking for the suit?

Don't be afraid to doubt your partner's bid in this vulnerability situation. Such a reasonable doubt indicates a willingness to co-operate with him, rather than the opposite.

Our last exhibit:

North-South vulnerable, and you are still West with:

3. ♠ Q 4 2   ♡ K 6 3   ◇ 7 4 2   ♣ K 7 5 2

NORTH	EAST	SOUTH	WEST
1◇	1♠	2NT	Pass
3NT	Pass	Pass	?

Pass. Again, credit the vulnerable opponents with the cards indicated by their bids. At the same time, allow partner leeway for aggressive action at the one-level. However, this is as good a time as any to emphasize again that you must play your players. If partner is the Rock of Gibraltar on his overcalls and North (or South) is the type who "came to bid," why then double away. This is a case of choosing the "table" bid in preference to the "book" bid.

With a real dud partner, you must expect to lose in the long run (unless the opponents are also duds). If you fight the inevitable, tooth and nail, you only increase your loss. And if you've cut a competent partner and have the stronger team, the sagest advice I can give you is this: don't try to murder the enemy no matter how weak they may be. Let them get into the wrong contracts on their own; don't tamper with their ability to play their cards poorly and defend badly. This will add up to a handsome profit over the long term, if you will just be content with it. But try too hard to talk your opponents out of their cards, and they will ignore you completely. All they see is the aces and kings in their hands, and nothing can convince them they are not pure gold. And though they beat themselves willingly enough —most of the time, anyway—they will not allow *you* to bamboozle them.

Meanwhile your competent partner *is* paying attention to your antics. If he believes your "tactical" bids, you may land in horrible contracts. If he begins to doubt your bids, you are on the way to losing your partner's confidence. Next thing you know, you will both be doing a grand job of fooling *each other* without making the slightest impression on the opponents. At this point you have thrown away your advantage of superior ability and are actually the weaker pair at the table. It's the hogs what get slaughtered.

Against an inferior team, you can take certain liberties, but these involve playing to their weaknesses rather than fooling them. Light overcalls may be in order, since weak players rarely double low contracts. You can relax your requirements for penalty doubles, as such opponents hesitate to redouble and employ faulty dummy technique. Bid some of the close games; often their defense throws you a trick or two. In brief, loosen up your bidding but don't go wild; extreme shenanigans wreck partnership harmony.

On the other hand, tighten up a notch against capable opponents. Stretching for doubtful games is taboo; aggressive opponents are quick to double and often follow through with a killing defense. Use discretion in making overcalls and in employing the rest of your bidding tools.

It is frequently profitable to tailor your pre-empts to fit the opponents' idiosyncrasies. Against a timid opponent, pre-empt more on bad hands, because he will go quietly. But give the bold opponent plenty of rope. Some players are goaded into action by a shut-out bid; cross them up occasionally by pre-empting with side strength, keeping the ax ready.

Your opponents have one thing in common with your partner: mistakes. You get gray hairs from your partner's boners, so it is foolish not to profit from the enemy's. The simple fact is that the team that makes the fewer mistakes is the one that usually wins. You can be a consistent winner without knowing a double squeeze from an eternal triangle—as long as you stay out of trouble. So, encourage the opponents to make all the mistakes they are capable of, and be gracious about letting them throw points your way.

This approach is particularly valuable in the play of the hand. As declarer, you ordinarily choose the line of play the percentages favor—the one that succeeds against most of the probable ways the opposing hands are divided. But against dull defenders, you should frequently choose a slightly inferior line of play if it gives them a greater opportunity to err.

Keep your ears open at all times. It is not only ethical, but good bridge to heed the extracurricular activities of the enemy. Their huddles and incidental histrionics impart volumes of information, and nothing in the rules bars you from using it to advantage. However, this is a case of "let the buyer beware." If you misinterpret an opposing emotional display, take your medicine in silence. You expect to gain in the long run by such "readings," and you assume you were not deliberately "coffeehoused."

Partner's mannerisms or intonations are something else again. You are expected to disregard any information you receive from this source.

Don't expect to be swindled. Practically all bridge players I know are honest citizens. As a matter of fact, as declarer you rely on that fact in analyzing the bidding and in ferreting out the reasons behind their defensive plays. And it helps you bring home many a shaky contract.

There is one final and crucial reason for studying your opponent: he may be your partner next rubber.

The Battle of the Sexes

I have been pounding home the theme *Know Thy Partner* for many pages now. But at this point I have to pull up short, for the next item up for consideration is the female bridge player. As far as I know, the man has not been born who really understands women. However, I must venture forth on this subject, because women constitute the majority of today's bridge population.

The most controversial question is whether men or women make better bridge players. Unlike physical sports, which require physical strength, a purely mental game like bridge should, in theory, not favor men. But it is significant that at the top level of bridge there is only one Helen Sobel for every ten or twenty reasonable facsimiles of Howard Schenken. In this super-expert range, the nod must go to the boys.

There are two good reasons for this masculine edge: More men make bridge a full-time career. Also, championship bridge demands sheer endurance. The important national tournaments usually run eight to ten days, with two daily four-to-five-hour sessions requiring intense concentration. Clearly, their stamina gives the men an advantage.

There is no such male predominance among average players. In fact, it seems to me that at this level women are the better players. The ladies are more likely to brush up on their game in odd moments during the day and get together for a session in the afternoon. Thus they tend to be better informed and more practiced than their husbands who, presumably, are immersed in the business of making a living and can seldom or never get away for an afternoon game.

Now that I have alienated all my male readers, I'll try to win back their favor by explaining to them the delicate art of playing with the ladies.

The fair sex seldom exhibits the male's competitive drive. Therefore, a man playing opposite a gal can bid a bit more freely to restore the balance. But he'd better not let her catch him overdoing it. What is it they say about a woman's wrath?

The gal is generally conservative, but the male tends to take chances—particularly the executive type who is looking for excitement and is accustomed to running the show. If he wanted calm relaxation, he'd be reading a book. He "came to bid," not to play it close to the vest.

The gal is gadget-prone. She's taken the trouble to read up on the latest doodad (it's the fad with her set), and she's darn well going to use it. So her male partner had better work out some compromise with her if they are to understand each other.

The clearest distinction between the sexes is in temperament. The man is out to win and single-mindedly attacks this objective (if any money is involved, it is usually incidental). Business is awful and his son has just been thrown out of school, but the only thing that counts at the moment is who has that queen of clubs. But the way the gal sees it, it's just a bridge game. She is out to enjoy herself and won't take kindly to a sharp rebuke for concentrating on her opponent's hair style rather than on topping her tricks.

There is nothing so desperately futile as a man's berating his lady partner. Either she hits back with a vengeance (and a *non sequitur*), or she gets that hurt look on her face and pouts. A man can't win.

Men may consider bridge a contest of wits, but most gals look on it as a social event. Thus they see nothing untoward in chatting about the latest scandal, next week's P.T.A. workshop, or their baby-sitting problems. If a man huddles too long over a bid, the gal may wander off to the telephone or kitchen. Her whole life doesn't stop for a mere bridge game.

If I have been on thin ice thus far, my ankles will soon be wet. I humbly venture that men are more logical about the game, and that women rely more on their intuition and emotional impulses. If a man leaps to six spades over his partner's opening one-bid, it may be a daring, strategic, or even stupid bid, but he thinks there is some logical reason for it. But a Mrs. F. I know makes the same bid to startle everybody. Then they will stare at her and at last notice her new Paris gown. If she goes down two tricks, it serves her male partner right for being so rude to her four hands back and ignoring her ever since.

Okay, now I've alienated both sexes.

HUSBANDS AND WIVES

When they start shouting at each other, you can be sure they are married —and will likely stay that way.

"It isn't as if that's the first time she's pulled that boner. Why, just last

143

week I read her the riot act for doing the same thing. What kind of woman did I marry, anyway?"

These scenes are not so unnatural as you might believe. You can forgive a stranger for his stupidity, but it is something else when the moron of the moment happens to be the *parent of your child!* Sure, husband and wife fume and fuss, but they make up eventually. And in the meantime, the bridge game has provided a good outlet for pent-up emotions. It may embarrass the other couple, but no real damage is done. There is only one recorded case of a wife shooting her husband in the middle of a bridge game. That was way back in 1929, and if he hadn't answered her back, he might be alive today.

Usually the husband remembers a bit later that the little woman is also a wonderful mother, superb housekeeper, and ravishing beauty, and this takes the edge off the argument. However, he still wishes she would remember to count trump and admit she was wrong *and he was right.*

There has been progress down the years. I can remember when the gal was never allowed to bid notrump, in deference to her husband's supposed superiority at this contract. Further back, she was even barred from the major suits. Imagine, if you can, imposing these shackles on the modern woman.

In all close questions, rely on the Golden Rule for married couples at the bridge table: "Do unto your husband or wife as you would unto any stranger."